INTENTIONALLY
YOU

INTENTIONALLY
YOU

Overcome Doubt, Silence Outside Opinions,
and Achieve Your Dreams

ATU CAMPBELL, CPRS

Intentionally You
First published in the US in 2025 by A&R Publishing Company,
A division of A&R Business Corp. LLC

ISBN: 979-8-218-75718-2
Library of Congress Control Number: 2025917439

A&R PUBLISHING
A division of A&R Business Corp. LLC

www.arpublishingco.com
For bulk orders contact us at:
sales@arpublishingco.com

This book is dedicated to my angels in the sky…
Monroe Perry, Dorothy Mae Campbell,
and Junior Lee Perry
I miss you and I love you…
You will never be forgotten…

And…

To all those who thought they could never
be all they dreamed of being.
You can!
Just remember…
Life is more than what is. It is what could be.

CONTENTS

PREFACE

Much of the information in this book has been around for many years. I have drawn from both the decades of knowledge left to us by the Great Thinkers and Achievers of the world, and from my own life experiences. This book is intended give people the ability to achieve their goals by giving them the confidence to believe in themselves. It offers to the reader an understanding of the underlying cause as to why people don't achieve at the levels they dream of, and it will help you learn to cast aside society's notion that you should live your life based on the opinions of others. Also, this book provides the steps that must be taken to develop an entrepreneurial mindset, which can help you achieve your goals, while overcoming the malady of low self-confidence. The main cause of underachievement is the fact that many people aren't comfortable being who they are. Most people don't realize that all the power they need is already inside them! This, in turn, causes them to fail to reach their fullest potential. I have personally internalized the philosophy of this book and used it to find my purpose and achieve my dreams. It is my dearest hope that this book of principles will impact your life for the better, help you find your purpose, and encourage you to do the things you never thought possible.

Sincerely,
Atu Campbell

ACKNOWLEDGEMENTS

First, giving all thanks to God, I would like to personally thank every person who stood by me through all the storms. This book could not have been written without your influence in my life. You supported me through every second, and for that I am forever indebted to you. To my parents who made me the man I am, who allowed me to become a free thinker... thank you. To my friends and family, who stood by me and encouraged me to keep going... thank you. To Aniyah, Carson, and Caiden... my babies, you are the reason I live. The journey of life, though it may be lonely at times, is one that you cannot travel alone. I thank God that I didn't have to. To my mother and father, Dorothy and Ronald Campbell Sr., to Myya, to my sisters Rukiya, and Debbie, to my sister-niece Aaliyaha, to my brother Ronald Jr., to my best friend Donald Kirkland, to Dyron, Henry, Chris, Tericka, to my brother-cousins Deontae, Kenny Jr., Cortez, to my second mother and father Aunt Lee, and Uncle Monroe... Thank you for loving me regardless of my flaws. Here is to many more years, books, achievements, and moments of joy. And remember, Legacy is the Journey we were all created to embark upon. I love you all, and thank you for loving me.

–love Tu

FIRST THINGS FIRST

To be clear, I am currently a productive upstanding citizen of society, just like I was when I got arrested on October 25, 2012. On that fateful day I had a car wreck in Memphis, TN that would alter the course of many lives, including my own. In the car with me was my youngest child, my six month old baby girl, Aniyah. In the wreck my daughter died. And my life changed forever.

Onlookers assumed that, because I was a young black male driving recklessly, I was just some "young thug," as stated by the off duty firefighter that was first on the scene. Without so much as a second thought I was labeled a monster. The DA's theory was that I had, in some way, had this accident on purpose to cover up the more sinister reality that I had deliberately hurt my own child. Nothing could be further from the truth. What they didn't know was that my reckless driving was due to me falling asleep behind the wheel, because of a glucose deficiency. Unfortunately, even when they did find out, it didn't matter.

It didn't matter that, at the time, I was currently enrolled in college, working for the city of Millington library, and also owned a small business. It didn't matter that I had never been in trouble before, and in fact, I had never even been to juvenile. It didn't matter that I had no priors, and no real knowledge of the criminal justice system. It didn't matter that, in actuality, I was a great father to my children, (at that time only Aniyah and Carson) which my daughter's mother informed the prosecuting attorneys of continuously. All that mattered was that I was a young black male, and in this day and age, that alone is enough to be considered a punishable crime.

Originally, I was charged with reckless homicide and a litany of other driving offenses, but due to defamatory statements by people, such as the off duty firefighter I mentioned, the DA upgraded my charges to felony murder. Like I said, in their eyes I was a young black killer trying to cover up a crime. After upgrading my charges I was assigned, with the consent of my lawyers, to a career offender's courtroom, although I had never had a single charge in my life.

Eventually I was convicted, although I never had a trial. My conviction happened by way of a plea deal appropriated by my lawyer and the prosecuting attorney who just so happened to be one of my lawyer's former students in law school.

On the day before trial my lawyer, who had been my attorney of record for six years, sat down in front of me in the court tank, and asked me, "So what did you say happened again?" I was incredulous, I couldn't believe that we were literally about to walk into the courtroom the next day and they didn't even know what my case was about! To add insult to injury, unbeknownst to me, they had called my family earlier that day, and told them there would be no court date. As a result, the next day there was no one there to support me, or to lend me any advice. I had no family at all in the courtroom.

Alone, afraid, bewildered, and facing a charge that carried life in prison without adequate legal representation, I signed a twenty year plea deal. My mother and father wouldn't find out about it until later when they saw my face plastered all over the evening news. All of a sudden, the youngest of my parent's four children, the promised child, the kid who had never gotten in trouble, who had never seen a prison cell before, would now have to endure twenty years of hard time in the Tennessee Department of Corrections.

Upon the signing of my plea deal, the news media painted me as a monster. They made it seem like I had all of a sudden decided to tell the "truth," and admitted to being guilty of the charge. But the truth was that I had no other choice. What they didn't know was that I only signed, because in the court tank the day before my trial, my lawyer told me that if I didn't agree to the deal I would do the rest of my life in prison. So I did. The news slandered my name, destroyed my character, and distorted the truth. Sadly, news outlets don't care if they get it right or wrong, or if the truth is told. They care only about ratings and sensationalism, regardless of who it might hurt, or how many lives it may damage.

For a long time I let this affect my self-confidence, which in turn, nearly led to me never releasing this book for fear of what people may think or say. Ironically, overcoming that exact fear is what this book is about: *not living your life based on the opinions of others.*

I wrote this book while in prison with the hope that it would help others tap into their inner greatness by over-coming self-doubt and silencing outside opinions. Why? Because, throughout my entire incarceration, I have watched men and women alike languish in defeat. The Department of Corrections does not , despite what the name may im-ply, "correct," but oppresses people. And make them give up on life. Even if it is not stated implicitly by the ad-ministration, the cumulative effect of some of the prac-tices of the Department's employees does just that.

I have watched too many intelligent people turn to drug abuse to assuage the pain. I have also seen people who, on the surface, seem to fare well in the environment, but upon closer inspection, they're struggling as well in their own way. I found that people like this usually resort to selling drugs, or gambling in order to earn money. Why do they do these things even though it can hurt their chances of going home? The answer is simple: They don't make enough money to survive, despite working thirty, forty, sometimes sixty hours per week. This is the conundrum inmates are forced to live in.

Most inmates are paid about seventeen cents per hour, which amounts to somewhere between twenty to twenty-seven dollars per month depending on hours worked. Without even factoring in the fact that the prisons continue to raise the prices on commissary, while refusing to raise inmate pay, twenty seven dollars per month is impossible to survive on. Therefore, due to their circumstances, many never realize the untapped potential inside of them. That is exactly the problem I wish to remedy. *Dismayingly, the malady of not realizing self-potential is not specific to people in prison; it is also a prevalent problem in society as a whole.*

My story is one that is unique. While I was writing this book to encourage others to live their truth despite what others may say, I didn't know that when it was time to publish I would experience the same debilitating emotions that I was trying to free others from. Ironically, in the writing, and subsequent publishing of this text, I freed myself.

Today, I am considered what some would call a justice impacted individual; however, that is not *who* I am.

I am a proud father of two sons, Caiden, and Carson, who are eleven and fourteen respectively. Also, I am an entrepreneur and co-founder of two companies: **Legacy Journey Group**, and **A&R Business Corp**. through which businesses I co-own a real estate investment firm, outside real estate holdings, and an independent publishing company.

When I came to prison I had $753.95, and from there I began building wealth through consistency, patience, dedication, and persistence. Although, I do embody these qualities and actively employ them to leverage my future, I must admit that none of this would have been possible without the unwavering support of my co-founders.

I wrote this book so that all people no matter race, age, gender, justice impacted or not, could tap into the unique abilities that God gave them, and live a life that is firmly rooted in truth. It is my sincerest hopes that every person reading this book succeeds beyond their wildest imaginations, and achieves everything they set out to accomplish.

Well, enough about me, if after hearing my story you are still willing to listen to the advice of someone who is perfectly imperfect; let's begin this journey.

INTRODUCTION

Success doesn't always start with privilege, opportunity, or a clear path. Sometimes, it begins in the darkest of places.

For me, it began behind bars where my freedom was stripped away and my future felt all but erased. Yet in that cold, desolate space meant to break me, something unexpected happened: I made a choice. I refused to let the injustice of a broken criminal justice system define or destroy me. Instead, the very place designed to crush my spirit became the birthplace of my transformation.

I'm living proof that your circumstances don't define your potential—your mindset does.

During my time in prison, I began a journey of self-reinvention that would lead me from incarceration to entrepreneurship, from hopelessness to purpose, and eventually to financial freedom. With nothing but time, introspection, and a growing hunger for something greater, I started rebuilding my life from the inside out starting with my thoughts.

Everything shifted when I realized that each person carries a unique gift—something powerful enough to impact the world for good. That insight lit a fire in me. I wanted to understand why so many people, despite their dreams, never achieve them. My search led me to a startling truth: most people fail to reach their potential not because they lack talent or opportunity, but because they're paralyzed by a lack of self-confidence—rooted in the fear of what others might think.

That truth hit home. It was familiar. I had lived it.

So I made it my mission to help others break free from that fear to silence the noise of outside opinions and find the courage to be their true selves. I came to understand that success requires more than skill or ambition; it demands the bravery to believe in yourself when no one else does. Only by overcoming doubt and letting go of other people's expectations can we rise to meet the full measure of our potential.

The methods and principles shared in this book are the very ones I followed to transform my own life. They took me from confinement to success, from hopelessness to ownership of my future. Today, I'm the co-owner of two thriving businesses and the proud holder of a growing portfolio of real estate investments. Yes, these ventures generate income but more importantly, they stand as monuments to a single decision I made behind prison walls: to change my mind so I could change my life.

This book isn't about quick fixes or overnight success. It's about doing the deep, sometimes uncomfortable work of reshaping your beliefs, reclaiming your discipline, and rewriting the story you've been telling yourself. The mindset principles that rebuilt my life are the same ones that will help you reframe adversity, develop lasting discipline, and build a life defined by purpose—not by circumstance.

Whether you're starting from rock bottom or simply striving for more, Intentionally You is here to challenge you, push you, and if you're willing to do the work guide you toward becoming the person you were always meant to be.

This isn't just my story.

It's yours waiting to be written.

Chapter 1

HAVE YOU EVER?

Have you ever found yourself sitting in a room, surrounded by people, and suddenly the thought hits you: "Why do I feel so out of place here? So different?"

It might be because you are different.

And that's not just okay, it's powerful.

There are times in life when we end up in places, around people, or doing things that don't align with who we truly are. It's a subtle discomfort at first, like trying to force a puzzle piece into the wrong spot. Over time, that feeling grows, especially when you try to speak about deeper things, purpose, passion, vision and you're met with blank stares or awkward silences. If you've experienced this, you're not alone.

The truth is, many people don't understand the importance of purpose. So when you talk about living intentionally or chasing something greater, it may sound foreign to them. They might even label you as "different."

And again that's okay.

People may tell you, "You're dreaming too big." But more often than not, it's not that your dreams are too big it's that theirs are too small. Their limited ambition usually stems from deep-rooted feelings of inadequacy. And here's the tricky part: as humans, we crave connection. We want to belong. So instead of challenging those low expectations, we stay silent. We downplay our vision. We conform just to fit in.

Why do we do this?

Because most people, whether they admit it or not, just want to be accepted. To be liked. To be seen as "cool." But in trying to be accepted by everyone else, we often reject our truest selves.

THE WORD "COOL"

There's something ironic about the way we use the word cool especially when we use it to describe something or someone as impressive, admirable, or desirable. In reality, cool is a misnomer. The actual definition of the word includes being indifferent, unfriendly, or even impudent. And impudence? That means showing a blatant disregard for others.

These aren't traits to aspire to but they are traits we often learn.

From early childhood, we begin to absorb social cues about acceptance and belonging. And over time, these learned behaviors the indifference, the aloofness, the disregard start to surface more clearly, especially in adolescence and early adulthood. For some people, these patterns become so ingrained that they carry them throughout life. The need to fit in, to be seen as "cool," becomes a silent force steering their choices, limiting their growth.

But here's the truth: breaking free from the need to fit in is one of the most liberating things you can do. In fact, it's essential if you want to achieve the kind of success you dream about.

Think back to high school. Most of us can easily picture the so-called "cool" kids a select group who only associated with others in their accepted social circle. Anyone outside of that circle? Ignored, mocked, or bullied. The "cool" status often came at the expense of kindness, empathy, and individuality. Those who didn't dress the same, speak the same, or act the same were treated as outsiders. And the most troubling part? That behavior of shaming others for being different was not only tolerated but glorified.

While this high school example may seem simplistic, it clearly illustrates the flawed logic behind our cultural obsession with being "cool." The idea that it's admirable to belong to a group where it's acceptable to mistreat others is not only misguided it's harmful.

And this isn't just a teenage problem. It's a deeply embedded social issue that extends into adulthood and society at large.

A LOOK FROM OUTSIDE THE CIRCLE

And you...

You start dressing a little more like them.

You try to talk like them.

Not because you admire them but because deep down, you're afraid. Afraid of becoming the next person they laugh at. Day after day, you find yourself wasting energy just trying to avoid being the butt of their jokes.

You laugh at things that don't amuse you just to be accepted.

You smile when you see them, even though their presence makes your stomach churn.

You show up to their parties when invited, not because you want to be there, but because you don't want to be left out.

And then... something shifts.

A voice whispers inside you. Quiet at first.

But over time, that whisper turns into a scream:

"I HATE WHO I'M PRETENDING TO BE! WHY CAN'T I JUST BE ME?"

Let me let you in on a secret...

You're not the only one who feels this way.

Most people live their lives conforming shaped by the opinions of others, paralyzed by the fear of judgment. They push down their own desires, mute their own voice, and abandon what brings them joy… all for the sake of fitting in.

Now here's another secret…

It doesn't matter what other people think.

And in the next section, I'm going to show you exactly how to break free from that burden.

But first let's talk about why their opinions don't matter in the first place.

NO HARD FEELINGS, CHOOSE YOU

What other people think of you has no real, lasting impact on your life. Their opinions don't shape your future. They don't have to live with the consequences of your decisions you do.

So, if we're thinking logically: Why would you let someone who won't bear the weight of your outcomes influence your choices?

It sounds obvious. And yet, people allow the opinions of others to shape their lives every single day.

Here's a truth that's hard to accept but necessary: most of the people in your life right now won't be there ten years from now. And those who do remain should be the ones whose goals, values, and vision are in harmony with your own. Why? Because we tend to emulate the people we're closest to. We naturally absorb their habits, their outlook, and their standards.

If you're striving to grow, imitating people whose lives aren't aligned with that growth will only hold you back.

Now, let me be clear: I'm not saying you should only associate with people who look like you, act like you, or share the same background. That's not growth that's comfort. What I am saying is this: if someone in your life is a hindrance to your progress or a threat to your peace, they should not have influence over your direction.

And more importantly, their opinions should not be your compass.

That might sound harsh. But this is the level of clarity and commitment required if you want to become the best version of yourself. Especially when someone's values and lifestyle directly oppose the kind of life you're trying to build.

For example, if your goal is to be an upstanding citizen, you simply cannot build close relationships with people who live in ways that compromise that ideal. And here's the part that hurts: sometimes, the people you'll need to create distance from are family, friends, or people you've known for years.

If that happens, be honest with them and with yourself.

Let them know where you stand. Tell them clearly that you cannot allow their choices or behavior to negatively influence your life. Some will respect your boundaries and want to stay in your life. Others may react defensively. Either way, you must stay grounded in your truth. Do what's best for you, even if it's uncomfortable.

I won't lie it won't be easy at first. But in time, you'll realize it was necessary. Because the journey we're about to take isn't for the faint of heart.

You'll need grit. You'll need resilience.

And above all, you'll need the courage to trust yourself more than you trust the noise around you.

So steady yourself. Dig in. And don't give up.

No one can live your life for you.

No one can walk this path but you.

Silence the outside opinions. Refuse to let anyone else hold the pen while you write your story.

Before we move forward, I want to share the most profound truth I've ever learned:

True power is the courage to unapologetically be who you are regardless of what anyone else thinks.

That is what it means to be Intentionally You.

SELF-CONFIDENCE

Chapter **2**

SELF-CONFIDENCE

T hroughout history, countless people have dreamed
of achieving greatness of rising above their current
circumstances and reaching for something more.
But despite the number of dreamers, only a relatively small
few ever succeed in making those dreams a reality.

That intrigued me.

Why do so many aspire, yet so few achieve?

I spent countless hours searching for the answer. And
what I discovered was surprisingly simple:

The underlying cause of underachievement, more often
than not, is a lack of self-confidence.

In the introduction, we explored how damaging it can
be to live by the opinions of others. And here's where that
connects: low self-confidence is deeply tied to the habit of
surrendering control of your life to other people. The two
are inseparable.

A person with low self-confidence doesn't trust their own judgment, which makes them more vulnerable to outside voices. That lack of inner trust can stem from various sources: past emotional wounds, unresolved trauma, social anxiety, negative self-image. Whatever the origin, the result is the same: hesitation, indecision, and fear of action.

Instead of confidently making clear, thoughtful decisions, someone with low self-confidence second-guesses themselves at every turn. They live in a constant state of uncertainty, unsure of their abilities and overly influenced by what others might think. That indecision becomes a silent dream-killer.

If you're reading this book, I believe you're someone who is serious about living a life of impact, a life of intentional success. And that means one thing: You cannot afford to fall into the trap of low self-confidence.

Why?

Because once you do, you start settling. You choose comfort over calling. You hesitate, you stall, and eventually, you stop trying. You begin living a life not of progress, but of what ifs.

And that's not living at all.

That's merely existing.

When a person lives in a constant state of indecision paralyzed by the fear of taking action they eventually become trapped in a cycle of mere survival. Life stops being something they shape and becomes something they endure.

Each day becomes a battle, and over time, the struggle feels so overwhelming that they begin to blame their circumstances instead of taking ownership of their future.

Now, let me be clear: circumstances can affect your life. They have affected mine.

I'm not here to deny that hardships are real. I know they are.

But I'm here to encourage you to stop accepting your circumstances as permanent.

If you're dealt a hand you don't want, don't fold.

Deal yourself a new one.

Living a successful life isn't about waiting for the perfect conditions or easy opportunities. It's about choosing to take action—especially when it's hard. Yes, taking action requires work. It demands courage. But if you want to achieve anything meaningful, it's non-negotiable.

Sana Ross, renowned leadership coach with twenty-plus years of experience, wrote about the linear correlation between self-confidence and the work of achievement in the online journal, *The Science of Confidence*. In it Ross explains the significance of taking action in cultivating success. She asserts that there is a dynamic relationship between the two, which she calls the "Achievement Loop." Ross writes, "In my coaching, I've observed this loop in action. When individuals embrace confidence, they're more likely to set ambitious goals, embrace challenges, and persevere in the face of setbacks." Later, she expounds further, "Forward momentum often leads to tangible results, which further strengthens their belief in themselves." In other words, the more actively you work toward your goals, the more able you become to achieve them.

To reach your goals, you must learn to be proactive, not reactive.

What's the difference?

When you're reactive, life has to happen to you before you respond. You're constantly adjusting, constantly reacting never leading, never deciding. You have no defined path, no destination. You simply "go with the flow," but the flow has no direction. It pulls you wherever it pleases, and you're just along for the ride.

Yes, adaptability is important.

But if you're so fluid that you have no direction, you're not living, you're drifting. Success demands intentionality. It requires you to take life by the proverbial horns—to make things happen, rather than waiting to see what happens.

In other words:

> Don't let life happen to you.
> You happen to life.

THE POWER OF YOU

Have you ever met someone who applied to every available job regardless of what it was and then accepted the first one that called them back? I have. In fact, I've been that person myself. If you've ever witnessed this kind of behavior, then you've seen what it looks like when someone is operating without a clear plan or sense of direction.

That doesn't mean the person is lazy or unmotivated. More often than not, people are simply worn down by the stress of trying to survive on insufficient income. Over time, that struggle can erode a person's confidence to the point where striving for meaningful success feels impossible. In those moments, the urgency of survival outweighs the luxury of pursuing purpose.

Still, the key to escaping that cycle lies in one critical mindset: refusing to become complacent.

Growing up, my family didn't have much. Maybe you can relate. But here's the truth: your current situation doesn't have to be your permanent one. Change is possible, even if the road is long.

Sometimes, that change begins with doing what you have to do so you can later do what you want to do. It may look like working a job you don't enjoy while going to school part-time. It may mean working two jobs so you can save and invest in your future. Whatever it is, you handle the present while also taking consistent, intentional steps toward the life you want.

Even if you're starting from a disadvantaged place, your socioeconomic status is not fixed. You can change it. But first, you have to decide to change it, and then be willing to do the hard work required. I won't sugarcoat it, it won't be easy. Changing your life, whether mentally, spiritually, or financially, takes effort. The kind of effort that demands action, consistency, and unshakable commitment to your growth.

That is what it means to harness the power of you.

Success isn't just a goal it's a lifestyle. But to change your life, you must first change your mindset.

Because once you decide to do something truly decide you can do it.

KNOW THYSELF

People have become disillusioned with society's definition of success due to the way our current social construct is shaped. From an early age, most children are taught the same formula: get a high school diploma, go to college, and secure a well-paying job. On the surface, this advice sounds practical. But I believe it is fundamentally flawed because it fails to address the most important issue of all: purpose.

Whether we acknowledge it or not, purpose matters deeply to every human being. Yet too often, we suppress the inner voice that draws us toward something meaningful something that stirs our spirit just to pursue a "respectable" career or meet societal expectations. But instead of ignoring that internal fire, we should lean into it. Knowing our purpose gives us the self-confidence and drive needed to achieve true success.

Have you ever noticed how star athletes often exude deep self-confidence? That's because, in order to achieve at such a high level, they had to discover and embrace their purpose. Even if they face insecurities in other areas, when it comes to their purpose, they are clear and unwavering. That inner certainty gives them a strength and sense of identity that many people lack.

Every person has a purpose even if they haven't yet discovered it. And here's the key: self-confidence is directly tied to the ability to realize one's purpose. When a person is unable to live out their purpose, it often leads to a sense of failure and inadequacy. Over time, those feelings can erode their self-worth and confidence. This is the real issue: society not only neglects the importance of purpose; it actively discourages individual thought and self-discovery. People are taught to value the opinions and expectations of others over their own internal compass.

But you don't have to accept that. You must break free from these social constraints. Seek out your purpose relentlessly. And once you find it, do everything in your power to bring it to life. Every day, commit even just a small part of your time to actions that push your dreams forward. Your purpose is not a luxury it's your foundation.

DOING THE WORK

Remember, Rome wasn't built in a day. Likewise, you don't have to accomplish everything all at once. But you must begin by creating a practical, step-by-step plan. Doing so gives you the confidence that you're taking meaningful action toward your goals—and that's the beginning of doing the work.

When you know you're doing the work, your confidence naturally grows. This is the first step in silencing outside opinions. At this point, you begin to understand who you are. And when you know who you are, you stop fearing what others think of you. You stop fearing rejection.

You realize: rejection isn't real not if you accept yourself. Outside opinions lose their power. What truly matters is success and failure and to reach success, you must go through failure. So even failure becomes irrelevant, as long as you don't quit. Temporary failure is not the end.

Once you reach this level of understanding, you come to a powerful truth: there is no such thing as success without failure. And with that realization, the fear of failing fades. The things that once intimidated you will no longer hold you back. Everything becomes an opportunity to succeed because you now know that if you fail enough times, you will eventually succeed.

This is how you begin laying the foundation for the mindset of self-confidence.

We'll explore that more deeply later in this chapter. But first, let's take a closer look at the role of education.

EDUCATION IS KEY

We, as a society, have been conditioned to be subservient in countless ways but one of the most powerful tools used to suppress our potential is the public education system. From an early age, we're taught how to become workers, not creators. We're trained for employment, not empowerment. There's no curriculum for entrepreneurship, financial literacy, or discovering one's purpose. Instead, we're guided along a narrow path built for conformity.

Before we even understand what life is truly about, we're asked, "What do you want to be when you grow up?" Doctor. Lawyer. Firefighter. Politician. The question seems harmless, even encouraging, but it subtly limits our thinking. It defines us by occupation, not by identity. A better question, the one we should be asking is: "Who do you want to be?"

Asking who rather than what opens the door to limitless possibilities. When someone is encouraged to define who they want to become and then given tools and guidance to pursue that vision they're no longer confined to a handful of predetermined roles. Their path becomes personal, purposeful, and powerful.

This is where I believe the fundamental flaw in our education system lies: we've been looking at education through the wrong lens.

We're traditionally taught that education is a means to an end—a way to secure a job, earn a paycheck, or maybe start a business. But in truth, education is far more than that. It's not just about degrees or diplomas. It's not confined to classrooms or textbooks.

Education is a lifelong journey.

It's the relentless pursuit of knowledge and growth. It doesn't end when school does it only begins. The most successful people in any field understand this. They remain students long after graduation, constantly refining their craft, deepening their understanding, and adapting to change.

Take medicine and law, for example two fields where continuing education is mandatory. But this principle applies to every profession. If you aim to be the best at what you do, you must keep learning. Stagnation is the enemy of excellence. Ongoing education is not optional it's essential.

And if your goal is to live a life of purpose, not just productivity, then your education must evolve accordingly. Not to fit into someone else's mold but to become who you were always meant to be.

We, as a society, have been conditioned to be subservient in countless ways. One of the most powerful tools used to suppress potential is the public education system. In school, we are trained to become a class of workers—taught the bare essentials to fit into predefined roles. There is little to no emphasis on entrepreneurship, financial literacy, or the discovery of purpose. Long before we even understand what life truly is, we're asked the age-old question: What do you want to be when you grow up? Rarely are we asked: Who do you want to become?

This difference is more than semantics. Asking *what* limits the imagination to job titles doctor, lawyer, fireman, politician. But asking *who* opens the door to identity, vision, and character. When we shift the question and help young people explore who they want to become, we ignite something deeper. We give them permission to dream beyond societal boxes and provide a roadmap toward limitless possibility.

The problem isn't just the content of education it's the perspective. Traditionally, education is framed as a means to an end: a way to get a job or launch a business. But I believe education is much more. It's not just preparation for work it's preparation for life. Education should be a lifelong pursuit, not something that ends with a diploma. It's the ongoing journey of learning, unlearning, and relearning. It's how we uncover our gifts, sharpen our skills, and walk in purpose.

True success demands continued learning. In fields like medicine and law, ongoing education is required but in truth, every field demands it, especially for those who seek to excel. Education, in its purest form, is the fuel of greatness.

All too often, the scope and power of education are misunderstood and misrepresented. African American poet

Margaret Walker captured this truth in her timeless piece *For My People*, where she wrote:

> *"For my people lending their strength to the years, to the gone years and the new years and the maybe years, washing, ironing, cooking, scrubbing, sewing, mending, hoeing, plowing, digging, planting, pruning, dragging along never reaping, never knowing, and never understanding."*

Walker reminds us of a history marked by denied opportunity of a people stripped of access to education and, by extension, freedom. Her words are not just a tribute to the past; they're a challenge to the present. No matter your race, creed, or background, we must understand: education is not just a pathway to a good job it's a pathway to liberation. It's how we rise beyond being laborers defined by what we do and step into the dignity of being known for how we think and what we contribute intellectually.

Your mind holds the power to achieve anything when focused with passion and guided by purpose. That's the beauty of education. It sharpens your thinking, deepens your understanding, and moves you closer to your purpose.

Motivational speaker and bestselling author Dr. Eric Thomas said it best in *You Owe You*:

> *"Education is more than school; education is knowledge."*

"Education is important, but once you've got the education, it's got to be balanced with expression and excellence."

These two principles, expression and excellence, are essential to self-mastery. To develop confidence, you must learn to express your true self, operate in your purpose, and demand greatness from within. That begins with cultivating a self-confident mindset and that mindset is forged through education.

SELF-CONFIDENCE IS A MINDSET

When I think about the most successful people I know regardless of their backgrounds, professions, or personalities they all share one defining trait: a mind-set of unwavering self-confidence. While the dictionary defines self-confidence as "confidence in oneself and one's powers and abilities," this definition, although accurate, only scratches the surface.

To deepen your understanding of this vital trait, I'd like to share a working definition I've developed:

The self-confident mind-set is a habitual mental attitude in which you require no approval from anyone but yourself. This mind-set shapes how you interpret and respond to every situation in life.

Let's break this down further by examining the words self and confidence separately.

The word self is defined as "the essential person, distinct from all others in identity." This is crucial. It highlights the most important principle of a self-confident mind-set: your opinion of yourself is the only one that truly matters. Why? Because you are the essential person in your life, unique and distinct from everyone else. In other words, how you see yourself will always outweigh how others see you.

Before we move on, I want to pause and offer you a bit of advice especially if you're a natural giver or someone who tends to lead from the front:

Be cautious about giving all your energy to others while leaving none for yourself.

If you constantly drain your mental and physical reserves trying to meet everyone else's expectations or worrying about their opinions, you'll soon find you have nothing left for your own growth and well-being.

Take care of yourself first not out of selfishness, but out of wisdom. When your cup is full, you can pour into others more effectively. And ironically, putting yourself first in this way will also make you a better leader. Why? Because great leadership flows from clarity, strength, and confidence all of which start within.

And speaking of confidence, let's now take a deeper look at what that really means.

Confidence is defined as a feeling or consciousness of one's power the quality or state of being certain. This is the second pillar of the self-confident mind-set: you have the power to stop fearing rejection. In other words, you have the power to be certain of who you are and what you're capable of.

Now, let's bring both definitions self and confidence together.

You are the essential person, distinct from all others. And within you lies the power to be certain of yourself. When you truly understand this, you realize something profound: you decide. Not your critics, not your peers, not even well-meaning family and friends—only you can determine the direction of your life. No amount of external pressure can override your right to choose your own path.

A self-confident mind-set allows you to step outside the labels and limitations that society tries to impose. But let's be honest developing supreme confidence doesn't happen overnight. It's a process. Confidence grows in layers, through consistent self-awareness, intentional choices, and courageous action.

As your self-assurance strengthens, so does your ability to be certain of your value, your purpose, and your identity. Eventually, you'll reach a point where you no longer feel the need to hide who you are. Instead, you'll begin to embrace your full self, unapologetically and with clarity. That's the turning point when you stop performing for others and start living as the most authentic version of yourself.

This is where intentionality comes in.

Living with intention means making deliberate choices aligned with who you are and who you want to become. It's understanding that every decision you make contributes to the trajectory of your life. And when you possess true, unwavering confidence, you no longer chase approval. You move forward with purpose brushing aside unhelpful opinions and choosing actions that benefit not only your life, but the lives of those around you.

DON'T WALK IN MY SHOES

When I was sixteen and preparing to graduate high school, I faced a big decision:

Would I go to college?

And if so, where?

In my family, it was universally understood—you graduated high school, then you went to college. I had no problem with that. In fact, I looked forward to it. So, the decision to pursue higher education was easy.

But where would I go?

I had a few small scholarship offers from different schools, but I never seriously considered any of them. For me, it came down to two options: MTSU, where I could study Professional Audio Recording, or UT Martin, where I could major in Computer Science.

The choice seemed obvious to me.

I wanted to go to MTSU.

Around that time, my parents noticed I had a knack for repairing computers and believed Computer Science would be a more practical and stable career path. And sure, I can admit computer scientists are well paid. But there was one problem: working with computers wasn't my passion.

Creating music was.

That was the dream I never voiced to my parents. Ever since I could remember, I've felt that creating culture-shaping music was the reason I was put on this earth. So naturally, since MTSU had the top recording and broadcasting program in the state, I chose MTSU.

But I never went.

I ended up attending UT Martin instead.

Why?

Because that's where my parents wanted me to go.

My parents believed that a career in computer science was a far more realistic path than trying to become a successful music producer. And to be fair, they weren't trying to hold me back they were genuinely trying to help. They offered the best advice they knew, drawn from their own life experiences and shaped by what they believed was safe and secure.

But here's where many well-meaning parents go wrong: instead of helping their children uncover who they truly are and what they're meant to do; they project their own hopes and fears onto them. That's exactly what mine did.

They saw that I could earn a stable income in the tech field, and since UT Martin had a strong computer science program, the path seemed obvious to them. Logical. Sensible. Safe.

But there was just one problem, I didn't want that life.

I didn't want to simply earn a living.

I wanted to be rich.

Deep down, I believed I could create real wealth by giving the world the very best of my musical talent. I saw music not just as passion, but as potential.

The real issue? I never told my parents how I felt. I never voiced my dreams. I never made my own choice.

So, the choice was made for me.

That's why I'm sharing this with you, so you don't make the same mistake.

Back then, I lacked the self-confidence to speak up. I didn't realize that the decision was mine and mine alone to make. I was so focused on living up to my parents' expectations that I never stopped to ask what I wanted.

In doing so, I surrendered my life to someone else's plan.

What I hadn't yet realized is this: true self-confidence comes from embracing who you are, making intentional choices, and learning to quiet the noise of other people's opinions.

LONG STORY SHORT

Things didn't turn out the way I or my parents had planned. I eventually flunked out of college and went into the music business anyway

It wasn't that I didn't value education. I later returned and earned a degree in Business Administration. The issue was deeper: Computer Science had never been my choice. It was my parents' vision for me. And because I hadn't chosen it for myself, I couldn't commit to it fully. Without ownership, there was no passion—only pressure.

So yes, I flunked out.

And by the time I opened my first recording studio, I didn't have a penny to my name.

Literally broke.

I couldn't even afford food.

But I was the happiest I had ever been.

Because for the first time, I was living life on my own terms. I was finally pursuing my purpose.

For years, I had dreamed of owning a recording studio and now, it existed. But before that dream could become real, I had to make a decision. I had to listen to my own voice instead of the voices around me. I had to silence the noise of outside opinions and trust the clarity of my own calling.

I named the place Studio Memphis, a tribute to the city where I was born.

It was during this chapter of my life that I realized something transformative: I did, in fact, have the power to achieve my dreams. For the longest time, I let insecurity and doubt convince me that my dreams were nothing more than fantasy lofty ideas, out of reach and disconnected from reality.

But that was a lie.

I had finally discovered the truth: that by making a committed decision and following it with consistent, pragmatic action, anything was possible. Dreams weren't just for dreaming. They were blueprints waiting to be built with belief, effort, and persistence.

PUTTING THE PIECES IN PLACE

My initial investment was around $7,000. In the music industry, that's barely enough to get off the ground it's next to nothing. But what I lacked in capital, I more than made up for in determination. That $7,000 bought me the cheapest equipment I could find (all from Craigslist) and secured 500 square feet of worn-down office space near downtown Memphis.

Still, it was a start.

Within two years, I had assembled a small team of five and was earning about five times more than I would have working for someone else. By the age of 23, I was charging $100 per hour. I wasn't rich by any stretch, but I had something far more valuable: proof. Proof that my dreams weren't just wishful thinking. They were real. Tangible. Possible.

But more than the money, what I gained in self-confidence was priceless.

That's why I'm sharing my story with you not to boast, but to remind you that your dreams are valid, even when others can't see them. Especially then.

Still, let me be clear: I'm not saying you should reject help or ignore wise counsel. That's not the message. What I'm saying is this: you must develop the discernment to filter advice, to separate fear from wisdom, and to believe in yourself enough to walk your own path, even when that path makes others uncomfortable.

Too many people spend years living a life that doesn't feel like their own trapped in expectations, paralyzed by doubt. I know the feeling. I lived it. I spent years trying to make someone else's version of my life work, all while burying the truth of who I was and what I wanted.

Here's the hard truth: sometimes the people closest to us, even those who love us, unintentionally do the most damage. Their intentions may be good, but the impact can be deeply harmful, pushing us off course and leaving us to carry invisible wounds for years.

This book exists to interrupt that cycle. To help you avoid or recover from that kind of damage. And if you've already been derailed, take heart. You can rebuild. But it begins with one critical shift: developing a self-confident mindset.

That's exactly what I'm here to help you do.

UNTANGLING THE WEB

The best way to start building a self-confident mindset is by creating a thoughtful, intentional plan for how you'll achieve your goals. Don't get caught up in the fine details or worry if your plans might change later, they will, and that's perfectly normal. Life evolves, and your plans should evolve with it. What matters most is giving yourself a clear sense of direction. When you've written your goals down, you'll always have something to return to when you need to refocus or recalibrate.

Your life plan should reflect your goals, your dreams, and most importantly, your values. Stay rooted in what matters to you. Never compromise your core beliefs just to fit in with the crowd. For instance, my core values are family, community, integrity, and honesty. I believe it's my responsibility to provide for and positively impact both my family and my community. So, I wouldn't create a plan that conflicts with those values. Your roadmap should support who you are, not pull you away from it.

Be bold. When you write down your goals, write them as they are not as you think others will accept them. Don't water down your dreams to make them more palatable or "realistic" to someone else. Yes, doubt may creep in. That's natural. But while you can't always control which thoughts enter your mind, you can control which ones take up residence. Don't let limiting beliefs convince you to shrink your vision. Dream big—and then think practically about how to get there.

One effective approach is to break large goals into smaller, actionable steps. These mini-goals serve as milestones along the journey and help you stay motivated. Each step you complete brings you closer to the life you envision. Remember: Rome wasn't built in a day, and success isn't a final destination it's a way of life.

Let me leave you with this thought, which is why I emphasize writing your plans down: there's something powerful about transferring thoughts into physical form. In *The Science of Getting Rich*, Wallace Wattles says, "Man is a thinking center, and can originate thoughts. All the forms that man fashions with his hands must first exist in his thoughts. Man cannot shape a thing until he has thought the thing."

So many people imagine the life they want, but few take the time to write out a clear, actionable path to get there. Writing down your plan is the first step to making your dreams tangible. Don't skip the first step.

NEVER SACRIFICE YOU

The blessing of being you is that you are unique.

There is no one else on Earth quite like you and that's your power. Embrace it. Your unique abilities and talents can help you achieve heights that most people only dream about. Discover what makes you different, and own it with unwavering confidence. Remember: the only person who can fulfill your purpose is you.

Shut out the noise of negative thoughts and outside opinions. Use your mind to shape your reality. If you want to own a business envision it, plan it, write it down, and then put in the work to bring it to life. Then go even further: capitalize on it! You can apply this same process to a career path, a lifestyle, or any dream you want to make real.

The self-confident mindset is this:

A habitual mental attitude that says you need no one's approval but your own.

What you believe about yourself is far more important than what anyone else thinks.

Write this down and put it somewhere you'll see it every day, so you never forget:

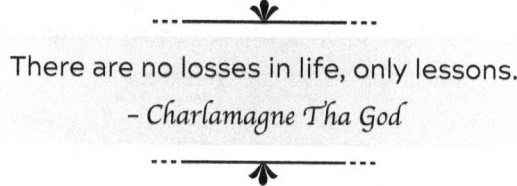

There are no losses in life, only lessons.
– *Charlamagne Tha God*

INTENTIONAL WORK

1) What key points from the chapter resonated with you?

2) Name three ways you can use this to improve you Self-Confidence.

3) How can you use your answers from question #2 to increase your level of intentional decision making?

4) How can this help you change your mind-set?

5) Write one goal related to changing your mind-set in the aspect of Self-Confidence.

ANTI-CONFIDENCE

Chapter *3*

ANTI-CONFIDENCE

Y ou're probably wondering, "What exactly is anti-confidence? Is that even a real word?"

Well, not yet. You won't find it in any official American lexicon for now. But who knows? Maybe someday it will be.

I coined the term anti-confidence to capture a specific psychological state that I believe needs a name. Here's how I define it:

Anti-confidence: A lack of self-confidence; the state of being unsure of oneself or one's abilities; a tendency to imitate others in search of external validation.

In the previous chapter, we explored the power of self-confidence what it is, how it works, and how vital it is to your growth. But there's another side to that conversation we can't ignore. Today's world often confuses strong self-confidence with arrogance. This misunderstanding can lead to unfair labeling and missed opportunities for both the confident and those observing them.

That's why I believe it's essential to unpack this concept. When someone wrongly labels another person as "arrogant," they're often reacting from a place of anti-confidence a place of inner uncertainty that makes authentic self-assurance feel threatening or unfamiliar.

By understanding anti-confidence, we can not only avoid these misjudgments, but also become more aware of the subtle ways it may be holding us back from embracing our own confidence.

YOU ARE NOT WHAT THEY SAY YOU ARE

Let's begin with a truth that needs to be made clear: self-confidence is not arrogance.

As you begin your journey toward building the level of confidence required for true success, people around you might start making comments like, "You've changed," or "You're acting different now." Some may even go so far as to call you arrogant.

Don't let those words deter you.

In fact, take them as signs of progress. If people notice a shift in your mindset and energy, it likely means your efforts are starting to bear fruit. Growth, after all, rarely goes unnoticed and it often makes others uncomfortable.

But here's the key: the average person is average for a reason. This usually stems from one of two things and sometimes both:

1) They don't yet understand what it takes to attain real success. Or,
2) They do understand it, but aren't willing to put in the work to achieve it.

In the first case, the lack of understanding isn't necessarily their fault—it just means they haven't been taught yet. And if they're open to learning and it doesn't hinder your growth, feel free to help guide them with the knowledge you've gained.

In the second case, however, the fault is theirs and the responsibility to change lies entirely with them. You are not obligated to carry people who won't even walk for themselves.

Now, when someone with low self-confidence encounters someone with high self-confidence, they might mistake that energy for arrogance. That's often because they don't understand what they're witnessing. In some cases, people project labels like "arrogant" to protect their own self-image and avoid feeling inferior.

But here's what they fail to see: it is precisely a person's supreme confidence that enables them to trust their abilities, defy limitations, and overcome deeply rooted mental barriers. It's not arrogance it's power rightly understood.

Still, not everyone mislabels confidence out of igno-rance. Some do it intentionally, because they resent what that confidence represents. They know that a truly confi-dent person cannot be easily manipulated or controlled. And that makes them uncomfortable.

Of course, as with any kind of power, confidence can be misused. That's a reality we can't ignore. But when used with self-awareness and purpose, supreme confidence be-comes an unstoppable force for personal growth and impact.

Which brings us to the next important concept: anti-confidence the mental state that stands in direct op-position to self-belief.

Those who wish to misuse you know that, once your level self-confidence reaches this level, you will no longer be able to be controlled with the fear of fitting in. Therefore, in pursuit of control, they attack it. They do so by purposely labeling others as, "acting different," or "arrogant," as a way to convince them to conform to the behavior desired by the accuser. This type of manipulation happens throughout all stages of life, although it is most often associated with young adults and teenagers in the form of peer pressure.

THE ISSUE AT HAND

Humans are inherently social beings. From the dawn of time, our survival has depended on our ability to form bonds and gather in groups. In prehistoric times, this instinct often meant the difference between life and death. Today, while the stakes may not be as dire, our need to connect remains strong. We tend to surround ourselves with people who share similar interests, experiences, or mindsets.

At its best, this tendency to connect and mirror others can be supportive and encouraging. At its worst, it can hinder growth—especially when we unconsciously begin to adopt limiting beliefs or behaviors from those around us.

This mimicry is known scientifically as emulation, though most of us recognize it simply as "fitting in." Emulation in itself isn't good or bad; it depends entirely on what is being copied. If you surround yourself with driven, confident, and disciplined people, chances are you'll begin to reflect those same traits. But if your environment is marked by apathy, fear, or self-doubt, it's easy to absorb those patterns too—often without even realizing it.

It's a widely accepted idea that many criminal behaviors, for example, are not innate but learned. In communities marked by poverty, trauma, or dysfunction, children often grow up internalizing the norms of their surroundings. This is why the phrase "a product of your environment" holds such weight. And while it's not always true across the board, it is a pattern frequently seen in both psychological and sociological studies.

Now, let's connect this back to anti-confidence. Imagine a person growing up or living in an environment dominated by individuals who lack self-belief. Their ideas are often dismissed, their dreams ridiculed, and their value questioned. Over time, without realizing it, they begin to mirror the same insecurities and doubts. They seek validation through others rather than learning to trust themselves. This is anti-confidence in action—and emulation is often its carrier.

To make this more relatable, let's consider an allegorical story. This simple scenario will show how anti-confidence and emulation can feed off each other—and how failing to recognize this cycle can quietly sabotage someone's future.

JUSTIN AND BRETT

Justin was a middle-class young adult who lived with both his mother and father. His father was a successful entrepreneur who owned a marketing firm, and his mother was a practicing doctor. On the surface, Justin's life appeared stable, structured, and filled with opportunity.

Justin's closest friend, Brett, came from a similar background. He, too, had both parents at home. They loved him deeply and worked hard to provide a good life for him. But their demanding careers often kept them away for extended periods—sometimes days at a time. Although Brett appreciated their sacrifices, he often felt a deep, gnawing loneliness.

That emptiness began to breed frustration and, eventually, a quiet anger he didn't know how to process.

In an attempt to numb the void, Brett experimented with drugs. At first, it was just curiosity. But the temporary high gave him something he hadn't felt in a long time escape. Relief. Comfort. And before long, what started as a release became a dependency. Brett's drug habit spiraled, leading him down a darker path, hidden from view.

Unaware of what was going on behind the scenes, Justin remained close with Brett. They had been best friends since toddlerhood inseparable, like brothers. They were both accepted into the same university and were preparing to start in the fall. From the outside, everything seemed to be going as planned.

Justin had noticed subtle changes Brett's slipping GPA, his occasional mood swings—but he chalked it up to senior-year burnout. Nothing too alarming. He never imagined his friend was caught in something deeper.

One afternoon, Brett invited Justin over to hang out and play video games. It was a regular weekend ritual. As they sat in Brett's room, controllers in hand, the laughter and competition flowed as always. But then, mid-game, Brett reached into his drawer and pulled out a small bag.

"Here," Brett said casually, extending the bag toward Justin.

Justin instinctively reached out, but as soon as he saw what it was, he snapped his hand back like it had touched fire. His face froze in shock.

"Bro, why are you acting so scary?" Brett asked, a smirk on his face, clearly amused. Justin stared at him, uneasy. After a moment, he finally spoke.

"Brett... what are you doing with that?"

"What do you think I'm doing with it?" Brett shot back, smirking, sarcasm laced in his voice.

"Here, try one," he said, pushing the bag toward Justin's face.

"No!" Justin snapped, his voice sharp, eyes wide. He couldn't believe what he was seeing.

Brett stared back at him, but his eyes held disgust instead of surprise.

"Suit yourself," he muttered, then casually poured the contents of the bag into his mouth.

Justin sat frozen in silence as Brett tossed passive-aggressive comments at him.

"You think you're better than me, huh?"

"So now you're too good to hang out with regular people?"

Eventually, Justin had enough. He stood and stormed out. The irony hit hard—Brett had just done something neither of them had ever touched, yet he was accusing Justin of changing.

Justin never told anyone what had happened. Brett was still his best friend, even if things had shifted. They stopped hanging out as much, barely talked. But when Justin saw him around school, Brett seemed fine.

That brought him a bit of comfort. Maybe things weren't as bad as they seemed. Honestly, Justin just wanted his friend back.

A few months passed. Slowly, they started talking again. Then, one afternoon, Brett invited him over to play video games just like old times.

And just like before, Brett pulled out the bag.

Only this time, things were different.

This time, Justin hesitated.

He didn't want to offend Brett again like he did the last time. He didn't want to seem like he thought he was better. So, he let Brett hand him one.

This time, he put it in his mouth.

Swallowed it.

This time, he let his fear of Brett's opinion steer his choice.

This time, he let someone else's approval rewrite the direction of his life.

Forever.

ANALYZE THE WHY

The story of Justin and Brett was intentionally simple, something even a child could grasp, so that the powerful principle it reveals would be clear to everyone. In the scenario,

Brett ultimately convinces Justin to take drugs. But the real question is: How?

The answer is a concept I call anti-confidence.

One of the key traits of anti-confidence is the tendency to mimic others in search of validation. And that's exactly what Justin did. He ignored his own instincts and values in order to gain approval from someone he considered a friend. That one decision seemingly small in the moment changed the trajectory of his life.

Sadly, this is not rare. People make the same kind of mistake every day. From schoolyards to boardrooms, millions have walked away from their dreams—not because they lacked talent or opportunity, but because they were too worried about what others would think.

In Brett's case, the manipulation was intentional. He used anti-confidence as a tool to guilt Justin into compliance. By throwing accusations like "You think you're better than me" or "You're too good to hang with us now," Brett wasn't just talking, he was pressuring. He painted Justin as disloyal, different, and disconnected. And Justin, still craving connection and affirmation, gave in.

That's why I emphasized, early on, the importance of building supreme confidence. Without it, you're vulnerable to external influence easily swayed by opinions, guilt, or peer pressure. But when you've developed supreme confidence, you no longer need approval from anyone outside of yourself.

It takes real strength to go against the crowd to stand firm when others mock, question, or shame you. Justin didn't have that strength yet. The moment Brett challenged him, his confidence cracked. And as soon as he began to doubt himself, he chose assimilation over authenticity.

This is how anti-confidence steals futures quietly, through moments of hesitation, guilt, and insecurity.

Don't let it happen to you.

Most of the time, people don't even realize when they're contributing to someone else's experience of anti-confidence. But whether it's intentional or not, undermining another person's self-belief directly or indirectly is a form of bullying. And the consequences of this kind of bullying are far-reaching. Countless people end up living lives that don't reflect who they truly are unhappy, unfulfilled, and disconnected from their purpose.

Sadly, this behavior is everywhere: in schools, homes, workplaces, and social circles. It's likely you've already faced it or will face it at some point. When that time comes, my hope is that this book has equipped you with the awareness to recognize it and the strength to rise above it with supreme confidence.

That's the heart of this chapter and of this book.

I want you to be prepared for those moments when the world challenges your identity. I want you to have the tools to stay rooted in your truth, to be intentional about honoring who you are, and to confidently walk in your unique gifts and talents.

You were divinely created on purpose and for a purpose.

Having supreme confidence means more than just being proud of who you are. It means putting your uniqueness to work. Use your talents to build something meaningful a business, a career, a mission. Let your authenticity become your strength. Make it your daily mission to live as genuinely as possible, no matter what others think or say.

That is the true path to success.

Write this statement down. Place it somewhere you'll see it every day so it stays with you:

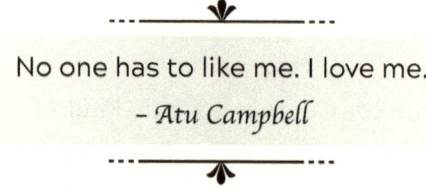

No one has to like me. I love me.

– Atu Campbell

INTENTIONAL WORK

1) What key points from the chapter resonated with you?

2) Name three ways you can use this to help you defeat Anti-Confidence.

3) How can you use your answers from question #2 to increase your level of intentional decision making?

4) How can this help you change your mind-set?

5) Write one goal related to changing your mind-set in the aspect of Anti-Confidence.

CAPITALIZE ON THE DIFFERENCE

Chapter 4

CAPITALIZE ON
THE DIFFERENCE

People have built entire businesses, and careers around their unique talents and abilities. This is the essence of what it means to *capitalize on the difference*. In order to use your unique abilities to your advantage, you have to first come to the realization that they are an advantage, not a hindrance.

RECOGNIZE THE DIFFERENCE

Dan Sullivan, founder and president of *The Strategic Coach*, teaches a trademarked concept program that he calls *Unique Ability*®. He utilizes the concept as a way of describing, "a powerful force that is at the very core of who you are as an individual." Scott Addis, spoke on the importance of identifying this powerful force in the online article, *Discover Your*

Natural Strengths. In the article he writes that your unique ability is made up of four characteristics:

1) It is a superior ability you have that other people notice and value.
2) You love doing it and want to do it as much as possible.
3) It is energizing for you and others around you.
4) You keep getting better at it.

"Most individuals are not able to identify their *Unique Ability,* let alone concentrate on it, because they are trapped by childhood training. We learn at a young age that the secret to success in life is working on our weaknesses. Unfortunately this focus on weaknesses creates a sense of inadequacy, failure and guilt."

Helping you unlearn that behavior is the focus of this chapter.

In order to use your unique abilities to your advantage you must begin by:

Identifying them and embracing them.

Sometimes, recognizing your unique ability starts with changing the lens through which you view your life. Your perspective shapes your reality. Two people can witness the exact same series of events and walk away with completely different interpretations because what we see is often influenced more by our mindset than the facts.

Take the classic example of the glass of water: is it half empty or half full? The volume of water hasn't changed, yet people can interpret the same glass in opposite ways. Why? Because it's not about the water. It's about the way we choose to see it. You can focus on what's missing (barriers, limitations), or you can choose to focus on what remains (potential, opportunity).

Let's dig a little deeper into this proverb. The amount of water is irrelevant; it serves merely as a metaphor. One person sees a nearly empty glass and concludes there's little hope. Another sees a glass that's still half full and recognizes a chance to build on what's already there. That small difference in perception is often the dividing line between stagnation and success.

Perspective is powerful. It influences how we respond to challenges, how we set goals, and ultimately how we live. With the right mindset, you can look at even the most difficult circumstances and discover a way forward. You can either be limited by obstacles or energized by the opportunity to rise above them.

There's a reason people say, "Perspective is reality." Because how you see things shapes what you believe, and what you believe influences how you act. And your actions, in turn, create your reality.

We've all experienced this truth whether we realized it or not. Let's reflect on how this plays out in childhood...

Think back to a time you got in trouble with your parents. Chances are, it all started with a thought. You had an idea to do something you probably shouldn't. You saw yourself getting away with it you believed you could so you took action. Then came the consequences. That single thought, rooted in a perspective, translated into real-world results. This is a simple but powerful illustration of how your mental lens—your perspective can shape your actual life outcomes.

Shifting your perspective is like putting on prescription glasses for the first time. Suddenly, you see things more clearly, and you're surprised by how much you've been missing. Many people go through life repeating the same patterns simply because that's what they've always done. But if nothing changes, nothing changes. As the old saying goes, "The definition of insanity is doing the same thing over and over, expecting different results." If we never adjust our thinking, our actions and the outcomes they produce remain unchanged.

Now imagine if someone never put on those glasses. They'd go through life unaware of the clarity they could have had. That's what happens when we never question our internal perspective. True change starts from within. You have to be willing to look inward before you can effectively respond to the world around you.

Take a moment and reflect on a regular day in your life. Let's use yesterday as an example. Walk through it in your mind: What decisions did you make? How did those choices align with your goals? Did the day move you closer to the life you want? Or did it simply pass by, full of unconscious patterns and missed opportunities?

Now go deeper: What beliefs are you holding onto that might be limiting your progress? Are there assumptions you've never challenged? Habits you justify because they feel familiar even if they don't serve you?

These are the kinds of questions that bring insight and growth. If the answers you uncover don't align with your goals, that's your cue something has to change.

Here's a simple but effective exercise to help you take that first step:

- Write down a few key questions about your day. For example:
- What actions did I take today that helped me move toward my goals?
- What decisions did I make out of fear, habit, or assumption?
- What belief guided my choices today—and is that belief helping or hindering me?

Answer each question honestly.

Identify one or two things you need to change based on your answers. These might be beliefs, routines, or even the way you talk to yourself.

WHAT'S YOUR WHY

Let's do an exercise.

For the purposes of this exercise, let's suppose most people spend the majority of their day at work, performing a series of tasks while there. The act of going to work would be considered the major event of their day, and the tasks and interactions would be minor events.

In order to do this exercise we must ask ourselves a series of questions. The questions we ask will be simple, but they will help you examine the motives behind your actions. The why behind your what.

Here is a list of questions to help you start the process of looking inward. **These are not the only questions you should ask; they are simply a starting point.**

QUESTIONS:

1) What is my motivation for going to work everyday?
2) Do I like my Job? If not, why?
3) Do I deserve more out of life? If so, why haven't I gotten it yet?
4) Do I know my purpose in life?
5) Am I doing all I can everyday towards actualizing my purpose, and realizing my goals in life? If not, why?
6) Do I care about other people's opinion of me? If so, why?

7) Does my life feel hopeless? If it does, why? Can actualizing my purpose and attaining my goals change that?

8) To what do I devote the majority of my thoughts? Positive thoughts of success or negative thoughts?

9) Do I realize that I, and only I, determine my success in life?

10) Do I realize that whatever kind of thoughts I give the majority of my time will become my reality?

CAPITALIZING ON THE DIFFERENCE

Capitalizing on the difference is simply this: *the practice of benefiting by turning something to your advantage.* The best way to capitalize in life is to control the thoughts that occupy your mind. Your mind is the only thing you truly have control over, and by transforming your thoughts, you can influence the world around you, and by doing so you can change your life.

Success is not a stroke of luck.

Success is intentional.

You have to think with, and act with *intention* towards a particular purpose, *fully expecting to attain it.*

I must warn you as I have before. Changing your thought patterns will change your decision making, and your change in decision making will result in a change of the people in your life. I don't mean to say that you will lose all of your friends, but you will lose some. The people you hang with, the places you frequent, and the things you do will all inevitably change. It is unavoidable. So be prepared.

In order to fully change your way of thinking, you must close your mind to all negative thoughts and comments contrary to your new mind-set. This is usually the reason for the change in your associates; because, not everyone will want to see you change, or do better. Shutting off your mind to negativity is a skill that is acquired through time, and persistent effort. It won't happen overnight.

Many people have capitalized on the difference before you, and many will do so after. So know that you can too. Don't miss your opportunity by viewing your unique abilities as a disadvantage. Don't accept other people's opinion of you. Realize your purpose, choose your path, and move with intention. Embrace who you are and capitalize on the difference!

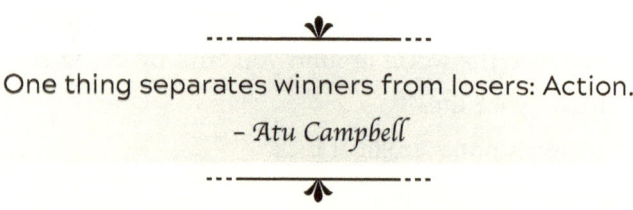

One thing separates winners from losers: Action.

– *Atu Campbell*

INTENTIONAL WORK

1) What key points from the chapter resonated with you?

2) Name three ways you can use this to improve your ability to Capitalize On The Difference.

3) How can you use your answers from question #2 to increase your level of intentional decision making?

4) How can this help you change your mind-set?

5) Write one goal related to changing your mind-set in the aspect of Capitalizing on opportunities.

HUNGER

Chapter **5**

HUNGER

Can you think back to a time when you were really hungry? Not just a little peckish, but stomach-growling, lightheaded, everything-smells-like-food kind of hungry. Do you remember how it consumed your mind? How you couldn't focus on anything else until that hunger was satisfied?

Hold on to that feeling because that's exactly the kind of intensity I want you to channel when I talk about chasing your dreams.

Let me explain.

When I say your dreams, I'm not talking about vague wishes or passing ideas. I'm talking about that one thing you feel deep in your bones the thing you were born to do. The thing you would do for free, every day, just because it brings you life. That's your purpose.

Now, if you're reading this and thinking, I'm not sure what my purpose is yet, that's perfectly okay. Finding your purpose doesn't always come in a lightning bolt moment. Sometimes, it begins with quiet reflection. Ask yourself:

- What makes me feel most alive?
- What kind of impact do I want to have on the world?
- What do I wish someone would create, change, or build?

The answer might be that you're the one meant to create that change. There are endless possibilities for what you can contribute to this world. Your job is to discover your thing and then go all in on it.

Which brings us back to hunger.

Hunger is the energy that fuels achievement. When you're truly hungry for something, you pursue it relentlessly. You don't make excuses. You don't wait for the perfect time. You don't stop when it gets hard. You want it so badly that no setback, no criticism, and no closed door can stop you.

That kind of hunger burns deep. It won't be quenched by comfort or convenience. And yes, you will face adversity anything worth doing comes with obstacles. But hunger is what pushes you forward when everything else says "quit."

You will fall. You will fail again. But failure is not final unless you allow it to be. Temporary setbacks are part of the process. When they come, and they will come, get back up. Keep going. Push yourself beyond your limits, mentally and physically. Hunger will carry you further than talent, education, or luck ever could.

Now listen, this type of unrelenting determination must be developed over time. You develop it by using the *3 keys of hunger*.

3 KEYS OF HUNGER:

- Key #1: ***Consistency***
- Key #2: ***Word***
- Key #3: ***Repetition***

NOTE: The first key, *Consistency*, must be used in applying the other two keys, *Word* and *Repetition*.

UTILIZATION OF THE 3 KEYS

The one universal trait among all living things is this: they must eat. Every living being needs to take in something to sustain life. Without nourishment, we perish. The same principle applies to your dreams.

Your dreams are living forms of mental energy. And just like your body, they require fuel. If you don't feed your dreams, they fade, weaken, and eventually die. You feed your dreams by meditating on them daily by keeping them alive in your mind, letting them grow, take shape, and evolve. But meditation alone won't get the job done.

You must take action.

Even if you're unsure of where to start, do something. Movement sparks momentum. A dream without action is just a wish, and wishes don't build legacies. So far, we've explored several essential components of a successful mindset: unwavering confidence, a capitalizing perspective, and intentional decision-making. Now, in this chapter, we add one more perhaps the most important of them all:

Hunger.

Hunger is the fuel of your motivation. It's the inner fire that drives you when everything around you says quit. Hunger pushes you to keep going through setbacks, resistance, and fatigue. It reminds you of your why—why you started, and why you can't stop now.

Now, for the 1st key…

CONSISTENCY

Consistency is defined as: *Cohesiveness, firmness, agreement or harmony in different things, uniformity of behavior, and resistance of movement.*

Quite literally all you have to do is look at the definition of consistency to understand what you need to do in order to accomplish your goals:

- **Be cohesive in thought.**

Create and maintain a clear mental picture of what your desire in life is.

- **Be firm in your faith**.

Be stead fast in the faith that you were born with the ability to achieve your purpose.

- **Maintain harmony in your actions, behaviors, and decisions**.

Your actions, behaviors, and decisions must be conducive to accomplishing your dreams. Negativity and underhanded methods are contrary to all things, and will cause failure.

- **Be uniform in your behavior**.

Be uniform in your behavior by doing all you can everyday towards achieving your purpose. This doesn't mean that everyday will be your best day. It means you cannot allow one day to go by without doing something towards achieving your goals.

- **Resist anything or anyone that tries to stop you.**

You must eliminate every obstacle to your success. That might mean distancing yourself from negative people even those closest to you. It might mean quitting harmful habits like drug use that could sabotage your progress. Whatever form resistance takes, you must stand against it. Success demands sacrifice.

Consistency is key.

And consistency isn't just about putting in effort every day. It's about staying committed through setbacks, failures, and doubt. It's about maintaining your focus, your discipline, your faith even when things don't go according to plan.

Setbacks are inevitable. But failure isn't final unless you allow it to make you quit.

Every failure carries a lesson. If you're paying attention, those lessons can help refine your path and improve your approach. So don't view failure as defeat. View it as feedback. Let every misstep inform your next move.

Now, to be clear: never giving up doesn't mean doing the same thing over and over, expecting a different result. That's not determination—that's delusion. What it does mean is sticking with your vision, and adapting with each new insight until you find what works.

Success will come if you stay the course and continue to evolve

In the end, consistency is doing your best every single day and staying in the game when it gets tough. Because opportunities don't fall from the sky. They appear for those who are prepared to seize them.

WORD

Now that we have discussed the importance of the first key, consistency, let's talk about the 2nd key: **Word.**

Words carry immense power. They can build or destroy, heal or harm, uplift or tear down. This power is limitless, illimitable. That's why you must be mindful of the words you speak and the words you allow yourself to hear. Every word you internalize shapes your thoughts. Your thoughts, in turn, influence your actions, behaviors, and decisions. And those decisions ultimately chart the course of your life.

In other words, success begins not with action, but with intention shaped first by thought, and before that, by language. Speak words that are aligned with your goals. Refuse to give life to negativity. I won't pretend it's easy. But with consistent effort and time, it becomes second nature.

Let me ask you a question: Have you ever told a lie so often that you almost started to believe it? Even when you knew it wasn't true? Strange, isn't it? The repetition somehow gives it weight. That's because your subconscious mind doesn't distinguish between truth and falsehood it simply accepts what it hears repeatedly. That same subconscious power can work for you instead of against you, if you choose your words with intention.

This is one of the great mysteries and one of the great gifts of being human. God has given us the ability to shape our internal and external world through speech. But this power must be used wisely, with honesty and integrity. The laws of nature will never reward deceit or harm. You cannot gain real success by causing others to lose. True and lasting value is created by giving value.

This principle is especially vital in business. If you want to thrive, strive to exceed expectations. Always aim to over-deliver. When you do more than what's required, you build trust, goodwill, and lasting relationships. And relationships, whether in business or in life, require harmony to survive and flourish.

Just as your actions can create harmony, so can your words. You've heard the saying, "You are what you eat." The same is true with language: You become what you speak.

Throughout my life, I've seen people talk themselves into opportunities or into disasters. I've watched individuals speak courage into themselves and step into greatness. I've also seen others talk themselves into fear, failure, and mediocrity. The point is not whether what they said was good or bad. The point is that what they said became real.

Don't underestimate that.

Use your words daily in a way that supports your vision. Remember, the more you hear something, the more you believe it. You can literally speak success into your life.

REPETITION

Repetition is exactly what it sounds like: it's the consistent practice of an action until it becomes second nature. It's about building habits that support and sustain the hunger mindset. To truly internalize this mindset, you must engage in repetitive behaviors that reinforce it.

There's a common myth that a habit is formed after doing something a specific number of times 21, 30, or 66 reps, depending on who you ask. But the truth is, it's not about hitting a magic number. Real transformation comes from integrating the behavior into your lifestyle. It becomes a part of who you are, not just something you do. That's where repetition plays its part, it's the bridge between intention and identity.

By now, the first three keys of hunger, belief, and repetition should begin to work together, forming a powerful, unified force in your daily life.

To put repetition into practice, start by creating a daily routine. Designate specific times each day for focused meditation. Choose a quiet space, free from distractions, where you can be fully present. During these sessions, center your thoughts on gratitude. Think of the things big or small that you are truly thankful for. Then take it a step further: visualize your dream life in rich, vivid detail. Imagine your dream home, car, career, relationships, don't hold back. The clearer your mental image, the stronger the impact (we'll explore why this is so powerful in the next chapter).

In addition to meditation, make a habit of speaking positive, life-affirming words throughout your day. Declare your purpose. Speak success over your life. Remind yourself of your potential and your progress. These words, when repeated consistently, begin to rewire your mindset and elevate your perspective.

This practice of daily gratitude, affirmation, and visualization not only conditions your mind for success but also builds resilience. It helps you see challenges differently less like roadblocks, and more like stepping stones. Plus, taking time to pause and reflect increases your productivity by giving your mind space to breathe and reset.

Structured meditation and affirmations should become as routine as brushing your teeth. To help you get started, here are a few practical tips to structure your day:

Try this: (1) Everyday you wake up, (before getting out of bed) immediately state out loud what your purpose is, that you can and will attain it, and that you will do all you can everyday to attain it. (2) Pick five different places that you are sure to look at everyday, and place a written positive affirmation there. (bathroom mirror, dashboard of you car etc.) Remember, each time you see an affirmation read it aloud. It may feel awkward at first, but it will become second nature overtime. (3) Every night, before going to bed, repeat the same words that you spoke when you woke up. (4) Repeat these steps everyday. Take the effort to make these steps a natural part of your daily routine. Eventually, the repetition of it will cause it to become your norm. And, as a result, it will become ingrained in your subconscious mind.

The beautiful thing about having set times throughout your day to meditate is it will serve as a time of balancing and re-centering, which is especially important if you're having a rough day. In the event that you do find yourself having a rough day, and it is not time for a meditation, you can simply close your eyes and pause…

While your eyes are closed repeat to yourself the reason for doing all you do. Remind yourself that you are working towards your purpose and that you can, and will, attain it.

Don't hesitate to take a pause, because taking the time to stop, focus, and re-center will give you a newfound sense of power, and allow you to push through.

In conclusion, I encourage you to strive to **be consistent**, **use your words positively**, **and repeat the process** everyday. The techniques I have provided are not the only ones you can use in your routine. They are simply meant to be a foundation upon which you can build. Make your routine your own. It should be tailored to your lifestyle. You can add to, or take out anything you choose. Do what works best for you.

As long as you stay hungry by using your words positively, staying consistent, and repeating the process, no one can stand between you and your goals. Just remember, you are a creator, just as the God who created you is…

Use this statement in your routine. Write it down and place it somewhere you will see it everyday:

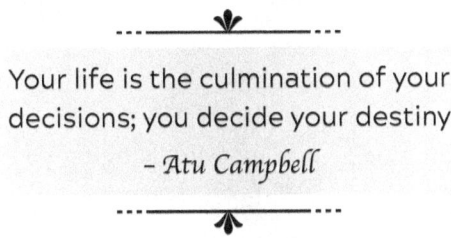

Your life is the culmination of your decisions; you decide your destiny

– *Atu Campbell*

INTENTIONAL WORK

1) What key points from the chapter resonated with you?

2) Name three ways you can use this to improve your Hunger.

3) How can you use your answers from question #2 to increase your level of intentional decision making?

4) How can this help you change your mind-set?

5) Write one goal related to changing your mind-set in the aspect of Hunger.

VISION

Chapter 6

VISION

D o you remember the quote I shared in Chapter Two on Self-Confidence? "Man cannot shape a thing until he has thought the thing." That statement holds a powerful truth: before you can create something in your life, you must first see it in your mind. In other words, the first step toward achievement begins with imagination a clear, mental image of what you intend to accomplish.

Take this simple example: maybe you dream of graduating from college one day. Close your eyes for a moment and picture yourself walking across that stage, accepting your diploma, feeling the pride and joy of that moment. That's vision in action. But in this chapter, we're going deeper. I want to show you how to use vision not just as an occasional mental exercise, but as a powerful principle made up of several essential attributes.

For the purposes of this book, vision is defined as: the ability to mentally grasp the outcome you want to achieve the ability to form a clear, personal image of what success looks like to you.

Your vision could be where you see yourself in ten years. It might be the path you believe leads to your purpose. Or it may simply be a vivid mental picture of the life you desire to live. However you define it, vision is personal, and it's powerful. The key is to not just imagine it, but to pair your vision with a practical plan to make it real.

Here's something to remember: the more detailed and vivid your vision, the more achievable it becomes. Your brain responds to clarity it helps fuel motivation, build confidence, and guide decisions. The fuzzier the picture, the harder it is to move toward it.

In the last chapter, I emphasized the importance of building a consistent daily routine. Visioning should be a part of that routine. Every day, take a few minutes to close your eyes and see yourself living out your goals. Visualize your success. Feel it. Believe it. Do this at least twice a day, once in the morning to set the tone, and once at night to reinforce your belief before resting.

This is how you train your mind to stay focused, resilient, and purpose-driven.

Vision is how dreams are brought to fruition. For example, a little kid may have a *dream* of one day becoming a professional athlete, but it is through *vision* that he "sees" himself practicing, and thus, goes out and does it. It is through vision that he "sees" the path he must take (high school team, AAU, college, then the pros). In the same way, you can *envision* a way to use your unique abilities to achieve success in your life.

Webster's dictionary defines vision as: *Something seen otherwise than by ordinary sight, a vivid picture created by the imagination, unusual vision in foreseeing what is going to happen.*

I love this definition, because it clearly sets forth the attributes of vision in several ways:

- *Something seen other than by ordinary sight:* This is the ability to know what path you should take to accomplish your goals. There is nothing ordinary about having this type of vision. That is why the individuals who are known for having "vision" are usually regarded as being extraordinary people. Think of the world's examples of extraordinary people: Lebron James, Steve Jobs, Martin Luther King, Jeff Bezos, and many more than can be listed here. Those with vision oftentimes become the leaders of civilization. They are the changemakers in economy, the titans of industry. That is why I stated that you should embrace your unique abilities. All the greats before you were unique in some way; moreover, they embraced it, and were empowered because of it. They were different, so they stood out from the crowd, and rather than be ashamed of it, they capitalized on it.

- *A vivid picture created by the imagination:* This is the ability we use when we *envision* something. This is where we create clear, vivid pictures in our mind of what our success looks like. Maintaining balance in all we do is important, especially in our visions. Therefore, when we imagine grand offices, homes, cars, beautiful children, prosperous success and material wealth, we should also envision our spiritual place of joy, peace, and happiness. If you can "see" it in your mind, your subconscious can internalize it, and help you bring it to fruition.

- *Unusual vision in foreseeing what is going to happen:* This attribute describes the visionary. Those individuals who see what others don't. Those who are willing to follow the path others won't. The ones who do what others say can't be done. Henry Ford is a great example of a visionary. Ford imagined a V8 engine and set out to build it. At the time, people had never imagined that this could be done. As a matter of fact other people, even his own engineers, told him it couldn't be done. Still, Ford plowed ahead. Because, he could see what they couldn't. In doing so, he eventually succeeded and essentially changed the world we live in. His invention has literally affected the lives of every human being on earth! You can do the same thing. Actually, you must do it. It is your duty to yourself, and humanity to make the most of your life. Just by you reading this book I know you can feel that **you were meant to be more than average**.

MAINTAINING VISION

On the flip side, a lack of vision or more precisely, the inability to maintain vision has caused entire corporations to fail. It's not enough to simply create a vision; sustaining that vision is just as critical. That's why many major corporations today are investing in leadership professionals to teach their teams how to adopt a "startup mentality."

The startup mentality is exactly what it sounds like: the mindset and energy of a newly launched business, driven by connection, ownership, and passion. It's an intentional effort to recreate the excitement, creativity, and commitment often seen in businesses birthed by entrepreneurs. What makes this mentality so powerful is that it brings with it the key traits of the entrepreneurial spirit: persistence, passion, grit, and, perhaps most importantly, vision.

Most first-time entrepreneurs don't start with wealth. In fact, they're often cash-poor. What they do have, however, is a clear and compelling vision. That vision becomes their most valuable asset. It inspires not only them, but also the people who choose to join them on the journey. Everyone involved in the day-to-day operations is fueled by the entrepreneur's dream of what the company can become. That dream becomes the driving force that pushes the entire organization toward success.

Big corporations have started to take note of how small, resource-limited startups are managing to achieve remarkable success. What they've discovered is this: those smaller companies are winning because they intentionally involve their people in the vision and direction of the business. That sense of inclusion makes employees feel like stakeholders, not just workers. They become emotionally invested. They take pride in their contribution. And that, in turn, fuels greater productivity, loyalty, and long-term efficiency.

Corporate executives have also realized a hard truth: the larger a company becomes, the easier it is for its original vision to get lost in the daily grind of corporate bureaucracy. And when a company loses sight of its vision, the result is almost always the same declining productivity, disengaged employees, and reduced revenue.

This isn't just a corporate issue, it's a principle that applies to personal success as well. Your ability to map out your path is fundamental to achieving anything worthwhile. And no, your plan doesn't need to be perfect. In fact, it won't be. Plans change, life shifts, and sometimes detours are unavoidable. But when you consistently lean into your vision when you learn to see your destination even when the road curves unexpectedly you empower yourself to adapt, adjust, and advance.

Developing and refining your vision is part of the journey. Nothing worthwhile happens overnight. What matters most is that you begin. Take the first step. Then take the next. Every step forward builds momentum. And here's the powerful truth: you don't have to see the entire picture before you move. Most people don't. But as you walk in faith and stay committed to the process, your vision becomes clearer.

Vision is not a one-time event. It's a skill you'll sharpen and expand throughout your life. As you grow, so will your ability to create more detailed and strategic plans. But don't wait for perfection. Start where you are, with what you have, and let the process shape you.

I've said it throughout this book, and I'll say it again you can accomplish anything you set your mind to. Look at my story. Despite incarceration, I found a way to build businesses that now allow me to create a legacy for my children. Was it easy? No. Did it happen overnight? Definitely not. And I couldn't have done it alone; my co-founders played a vital role. But what made the difference was my willingness to envision, to try, to fail, to adjust, and to keep going.

That's what separates the ordinary from the extraordinary.

Most people give up after investing time and energy into a dream, only to see it fall apart. But those who refuse to quit who keep showing up, even after failure are the ones who eventually rise above. The elite few who persist, despite setbacks, are the ones who succeed.

Honestly, there were times during the process of trying to start Legacy Journey Group that my co-founder and I almost wanted to quit, but we didn't. We intentionally chose to persist. We used the *three keys of hunger* to motivate us. We spoke what we wanted, consistently applied ourselves, and repeated the process everyday. I am no genius by a long shot, but I know what helped me, and I know it can help you too. Follow the steps in this book, and you will accomplish everything you want. Let's go over the steps we have covered so far:

1) Embrace your unique identity (Introduction).
2) Develop Supreme Confidence (which you can do, because you now embrace your true self).
3) Be wary of the haters (don't fall prey to Anti-confidence).
4) Create a plan to capitalize on your unique abilities (realize that being unique is an asset).
5) Develop your sense of hunger, until you burn with desire to achieve (consistency, word, and repetition).
6) Use your vision to help you see your path more clearly (envision yourself living your idea of success).

When you finish reading this chapter, I encourage you to pull out a piece of paper, and write down your plan for how you will accomplish your goals. Don't worry about creating a perfect plan; just get *something* on paper that you can look at everyday you wake up, and every night before you go to bed. Remember to use your vision to your advantage. You must use the eye of your mind to see what no-one else can, create a stark image of that vision with your imagination, and use your visionary power to carry your vision forward. Now let's turn our attention to dedication and why you need to be dedicated to your purpose so intently that you become obsessed with accomplishing it.

INTENTIONAL WORK

1) What key points from the chapter resonated with you?

2) Name three ways you can use this to improve your Vision.

3) How can you use your answers from question #2 to increase your level of intentional decision making?

4) How can this help you change your mind-set?

5) Write one goal related to changing your mind-set in the aspect of Vision.

DEDICATION

Chapter **7**

DEDICATION

Dedication: To set apart for a definite purpose, to commit to a goal or way of life.

Dedication is the secret behind every meaningful success. When you commit yourself to a cause, you carve out a sacred space for it in your life. Think of anyone who has achieved something notable every one of them had to dedicate themselves wholeheartedly to their goals.

Now, I won't sugarcoat it dedication demands energy, discipline, and a deep sense of purpose. But here's the beauty of it: when you truly dedicate yourself to something, you tap into the divine power placed within you by your Creator. This is the same infinite energy that fuels the universe. And yes, that power is available to you. With it, you can shape your life in the direction of your deepest desires.

Dedication is the spark that ignites your dreams and keeps them burning. It fuels the hunger we discussed back in Chapter Five the hunger to manifest your vision. When you make the intentional decision to dedicate yourself, it doesn't just clarify your focus; it strengthens your confidence and fortifies your motivation. It becomes the inner voice that urges you forward, even in the face of setbacks. It reminds you that failure is not defeat it's feedback. It's redirection. It's growth.

Without dedication, success is impossible. There's simply no substitute for it. And let me be clear—success isn't just a moment or a milestone. It's a way of life. It's a daily choice to show up and give your all. When you choose to fully commit to your purpose and show up consistently, you align yourself with momentum and momentum is powerful.

Now, let's talk practically. Dedicating yourself daily to your goals doesn't mean you must grind nonstop, 24/7. Some people do, and that's fine if it works for them. But many of us have jobs, children, and responsibilities that demand our time and attention. Dedication doesn't mean neglecting those things. It simply means that every day no matter how full your schedule is you carve out time to do something, anything, toward your goals. Even if it's just a few minutes, those minutes matter.

Of course, that's not an excuse to slack off. You can't expect to grow by giving your dreams crumbs. But on days when life pulls you in a thousand directions, show up anyway. Do what you can. Keep the flame alive.

That's what dedication looks like not perfection, but persistence. Not fixation, but intention. A daily decision to invest in your future, one step at a time.

You must create time in your schedule and cut out anything that doesn't align with your vision. That means letting go of relationships that don't share your values, quitting harmful habits, and uprooting negative mindsets. These things might feel difficult to release, but they are roadblocks that will hold you back. Real dedication demands clarity and clarity often requires sacrifice.

Once you've made a plan of action, commit to it with unwavering dedication, even if that means losing some people along the way. Everyone can wish for success but wishes don't build legacies. Only concrete plans and consistent, decisive action can do that. The average person dreams of success; only the determined see it through.

History doesn't remember wishers. It remembers the steadfast.

Consider civil rights leader A. Philip Randolph. If he and others like him had backed down in the face of resistance, you might not even be holding this book right now. Randolph once said, "Freedom is never given; it is won." And the same is true of success. It is not handed out it is earned through relentless effort and focus. There was a time when Black Americans were forbidden to read, let alone write. But through sheer dedication, generations shattered those barriers and claimed freedoms once thought unreachable.

Let that truth remind you: Dedication is not optional. It's essential.

Listen closely: Struggle is inevitable on the road to success. It won't be easy, and it certainly won't fall into your lap. But if you push forward through opposition, through setbacks and refuse to quit, you will be rewarded.

Opportunity doesn't show up for the unprepared. It reveals itself to those who are positioned to receive it. That positioning is not accidental it's intentional. It comes from carefully considering the decisions you make each day. Every choice adds up, forming the trajectory of your life.

When you choose to live with purpose and stay committed to it, you naturally place yourself in alignment with opportunity. Your unwavering dedication will become evident not just to you, but to those around you. People can feel it. They'll see the fire in you, the focus, the drive and that energy is magnetic.

It's that unmistakable intensity that will draw the right people and the right opportunities to you.

OBSESSED WITH DEDICATION

Dedication and persistence go hand in hand. Dedication enhances persistence; it imbues the mindset of persistence with a spiritual essence. The combination of the two creates a power that is so potent that, when applied to your achieving your goals, you become obsessed with success.

Can you think of a time in your life, that you were so focused on obtaining something, that everything you thought about was related to getting it done? If so, try tap into that place in your mind, because that is where you need to be mentally. You need to be obsessed with success.

Obsessed: to be preoccupied intensely or abnormally; a persistent disturbing preoccupation.

Now, I know you're thinking... *Abnormally? Disturbing?* **What**???

Don't let the definition scare you, but its true. Sometimes the truth is scary, and here is the truth: When you become so focused, so persistent that nothing can deter you from going after your dreams, people will start to look at you differently. You will no longer be "normal" to them, and actually, they will be correct.

Why do I say this? Because, ordinary people don't understand this level of dedication, which is exactly why they remain ordinary, and never become extraordinary. So don't be disturbed by their reactions, be encouraged, because accomplishing your dreams requires you to be anything but ordinary.

Take Henry Ford for example, people thought he was obsessed. In fact he was, but not in the negative way people usually envision when they think of obsession. Rather, Ford was persistent, almost obstinate, in achieving his vision.

Ford's vision was to create a single cast block V8 engine, so he hired the best professionals money could buy, even though all prior knowledge told him that it was impossible to engineer a single cast block V8 engine. But he was determined to try anyway. His engineers failed many times, and it is said that they approached him on many occasions and informed him that it was simply impossible to accomplish what he wanted.

But he repeatedly told them to try again.

Ford's engineers were extremely intelligent and adept technicians, but they knew little of the illimitable source from which Ford imbibed. They didn't factor in the power of dedication

Henry Ford was a visionary and a true titan of industry, but regardless of all he achieved, he was still a human being like you and I. If Ford, could harness this energy to amass great wealth and accomplish notable success, so can you. Ford was able to accomplish the things he did, because he was dedicated to his vision, and by harnessing this quasi-spiritual energy he made the impossible possible. Because of Ford's unrelenting determination, and dedication to his vision, he changed the course of history forever.

WHY NOT YOU?

Ever asked yourself what separates winners from losers?

The answer is action.

Always take action.

In today's world it's easier than ever to take action, because almost everything is online. This unique time in history allows us to use technology to our advantage. We can use tech to help us achieve our purpose faster, and in more unique ways than ever before. For example, social media has allowed anybody connected to the internet the opportunity to create content and monetize their lives (If they are willing to part with some or all of their privacy). We are able to connect with billions of people at the click of a button. I'm not saying you should go put your entire life on Youtube for the world to see. I'm simply giving an example of one of the many ways people are finding opportunities that were not available to us in the past. You don't have to be a social media influencer. You don't even have to like social media. But you can use it to effectively market yourself, your product, and your brand in order to increase the revenue you receive for the value you provide. Everything costs something, and everyone deserves compensation for the value they provide. And you are no different. Compensation does not have to be in the form of money. It can be anything from monetary value to emotional and spiritual enlightenment. You decide what type of compensation you require. Just remember that any value you provide should benefit everybody it affects, including you.

People get uncomfortable when it comes to talking about finances, because society has made the conversation about money a taboo. Sometimes its overzealous, misguided religious leaders that erroneously give people the impression that it is a sin to desire wealth.

This couldn't be further from the truth.

The desire to be financially free is actually noble. I say this, because in order to contribute the best you have to offer to the world you have to be able to take the time to explore yourself on a deeper level. But you can't if survival is constantly at the forefront of your conscious mind.

I am here to tell you that it is not wrong to desire to live life to the fullest extent, and in this world, you must have the finances to do so. Actually this inherent desire is natural at the most canonical level.

All life forms constantly seek to exist on a higher plane.

This is the way of nature:

Constant evolution.

If you are one of the people who feel guilty for wanting more for yourself and your loved ones, I advise you to break that mindset and replace it with a mindset of dedication and affluence... Others, such as Henry Ford, have enjoyed life to its fullest extent. Why Not you?

In *The Power of Dedication*, life coach, Creed Branson wrote, "The dedication to work hard is necessary for personal growth and ultimately to achieve our definition of success. Beyond the tangible rewards, such dedication plays a pivotal role in fostering self-awareness and achieving clarity of vision."

Dedication requires you to plunge ahead, even when you don't see the fruit of your labor in the present moment. You must believe, without doubt, that the work you put in today will produce benefits tomorrow. I won't sugarcoat it dedication demands energy, discipline, and a deep sense of purpose. But when you truly dedicate yourself to something you have the power to shape your life in the direction of your deepest desires.

INTENTIONAL WORK

1) What key points from the chapter resonated with you?

2) Name three ways you can use this to improve your ability to Dedicate yourself to accomplishing your goals.

3) How can you use your answers from question #2 to increase your level of intentional decision making?

4) How can this help you change your mind-set?

5) Write one goal related to changing your mind-set in the aspect of Dedication.

MAKE A PLAN & STICK TO IT

Chapter *8*

MAKE A PLAN &
STICK TO IT

D o you remember what we talked about in Chapter Five: Hunger, when I said that a dream without action is just wishful thinking? Let's take that idea a step further. Before you can act effectively, you need something just as essential: a plan.

Success doesn't happen by accident. The most reliable way to reach any meaningful goal is to create a clear, practical plan, write it down, and follow it consistently. Think of your plan as a roadmap. It doesn't just show you where you're going it guides you step by step until you get there.

One of the smartest ways to build this roadmap is by breaking your larger goal into smaller, manageable pieces what I like to call mini goals.

Each mini goal should be realistic, simple, and intentionally designed to lead into the next. Picture them like stepping stones across a stream. With each step you take, you're not only moving forward you're building momentum. You're proving to yourself that success is possible, one win at a time. That's the beauty of this approach: every small victory boosts your confidence, and that confidence becomes the fuel for your next move. It's a snowball effect, the more you accomplish, the easier it becomes to keep going.

As you move toward your goals, I encourage you to develop a daily habit that lasts just a few minutes a day. Sit quietly, close your eyes, and visualize your success. Imagine what it will feel like to cross the finish line. Just as we discussed in Chapter Five, using meditation in this way helps you stay grounded, focused, and emotionally aligned with your purpose. And when the inevitable challenges arise and they will this simple practice will reconnect you to your "why" and re-ignite the fire you need to press on.

Do this: Take the time to set aside ten minutes daily every morning. During this time read your entire written plan aloud, then close your eyes and imagine what your life will look like if you successfully carry out your plans. If your plans are highly detailed, focus on your major goals and the steps it will take to achieve them (again, this should only take about ten minutes daily). Don't overdo it, or make this time feel like a chore. This time is designed to motivate you by reminding you *why* you do what you do everyday.

FORCE MULTIPLIERS

Some people prefer to make their plans in private, often out of fear, fear that someone might steal their ideas or criticize them. If you're one of those people, I encourage you to reconsider. I once felt the same way. But over time, I realized that no single person has enough knowledge or power to build great wealth alone. That insight changed everything for me.

(Important Note: I'm not suggesting you give away your intellectual property. I'm simply encouraging you to seek help from people you trust when you need it.)

At some point in your journey, collaboration will become essential. You'll need employees, business partners, mentors, and others to bring your vision to life. This is where Chapter Nine: Choose Your Circle Wisely becomes relevant.

Here's my advice: Start by developing your initial plans privately. Once you've laid the foundation, share those plans with trusted individuals on your team and invite their input. Why? Because when you bring together multiple Finesse Types, (You will find out what a Finesse Type is in the next chapter. For now, just think of them as different personality types.) to collaborate on a plan, you benefit from a powerful synergy. This convergence of diverse thinking styles creates what I call a force multiplier.

Try it. You'll be amazed at what you can accomplish through intentional group effort.

RELENTLESS PERSISTENCE

As you begin making plans and writing them down, under-stand this: at some point, your plans may fail or fall short of your expectations. When that happens, the average person quits. But you are not the average person.

You will not quit.

How do I know?

Because you're reading this book.

When you encounter temporary failure, it's not a sign to give up it's a signal to rejoice and reevaluate. I know you might be thinking, "What!? That's the dumbest thing I've ever heard!" But hear me out: it's time to rejoice because you actually took action. Your plans may not have worked perfectly, but something did. That's progress.

Now it's time to assess what worked and what didn't. Identify the flaws in your plan, make the necessary adjust-ments, and try again. If it still doesn't work, evaluate again, tweak your approach, and go at it once more. Repeat this process as many times as needed until you succeed.

This phase of your journey may be mentally draining. But you must be relentlessly persistent. Why?

Because success lives on the other side of failure.

Train yourself to see failures as temporary setbacks. The only time you truly fail is when you give up.

No one in history has gotten everything right on the first try.

Every major success story is built on a foundation of relentless effort, persistence, and the courage to rise after falling. It doesn't matter what others think you're capable of. It only matters what you believe and, more importantly, what you choose to do.

THE PRICE IS RIGHT

If you forget everything else I say in this book, remember this: You determine your worth.

Let me share a story that illustrates this truth.

The other day, I called my good friend Donald owner of Lifestyle Screen Printing, a thriving business in Memphis, TN. Donald is like family to me. I've had a front-row seat on his journey, and I've witnessed the blood, sweat, and tears he poured into building that company from the ground up.

During our conversation, I asked him a straightforward question:

"Would you ever consider selling your company?"

He paused for a moment and replied, "Yes, but it would have to be a crazy number like $800,000."

I stopped him right there.

"Donald," I said, "that's not crazy at all."

Now keep in mind, Donald isn't just any business owner. He's a sharp, well-educated entrepreneur with a degree in accounting. He already knew his business had value. But sometimes, when you're deep in the grind, it's easy to lose sight of how far you've come and how much you've built. My reminder was simple:

Never underestimate your value—not for a second.

When you're immersed in doing the work, it can be hard to step back and recognize the greatness you're achieving. But others see it, I saw it. I saw the value Donald was creating, and I wanted to make sure he saw it too.

Whether or not my words inspired him, what happened next certainly inspired me.

About a year after that conversation, Donald scaled his business into a multi-million dollar operation earning more in a single year than the amount he once thought his entire company was worth. That transformation is proof of what happens when you believe in your worth and continue to build on it.

At the time, Donald was already delivering more value than he realized. But because he believed he deserved more and because he kept pushing to grow he ultimately forced the market to match his self-valuation. He didn't wait for permission. He placed the price on his value, and the world paid it.

And that's the lesson I want you to take away:

You place the price on your value.

Be sure that price isn't discounted by fear, doubt, or the opinions of others. When you're clear about your worth, and when that worth is backed by effort, consistency, and value you'll never sell yourself short.

Make the price right. And own it.

GET EXPOSED

Throughout this book, I've encouraged you to envision success in your mind. But I also understand that people can only imagine what they've been exposed to. That's why so many individuals born in underserved communities often remain stuck because they haven't seen anything different. In many cases, people in these communities rarely have the opportunity to venture beyond their neighborhood, so their worldview becomes limited to what they've always known.

This is why I urge you to intentionally seek out exposure to new places, people, and cultures.

Books and the internet are two powerful tools for expanding your horizons, especially if traveling isn't immediately possible. But if you can experience these things in person, I implore you to do so. For instance, if your goal is to own a million-dollar home, you need to see what that actually looks like. Visit open houses in high-end neighborhoods. Walk through them. Get inspired.

Why? Because inspiration fuels your imagination and that imagination feeds your subconscious mind. The more you engage with images, articles, books, and environments that align with your vision of success, the clearer and more compelling your internal vision becomes. This clarity is the first step toward forming a tangible, actionable plan.

Creating a plan means organizing your goals intelligently on paper so they can be carried out efficiently. Don't overthink it. Visualize it, write it down, then structure it in clear, sequential steps. And remember: it doesn't have to be perfect. Plans can and should evolve. Revise as often as necessary to keep them realistic and effective.

Don't get stuck in the trap of perfectionism. Nothing in this world is perfect, and chasing perfection will only leave you frustrated. Everything is subject to change. The only thing you can truly control is your commitment to relentlessly pursue your purpose.

Your dreams are closer than you think. All you have to do is make a plan and stick to it.

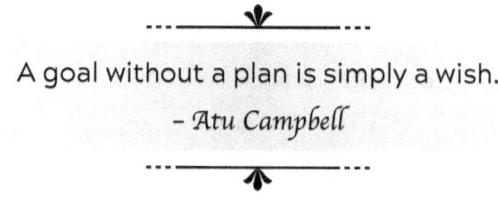

A goal without a plan is simply a wish.

– *Atu Campbell*

INTENTIONAL WORK

1) What key points from the chapter resonated with you?

2) Name three ways you can use this to improve your ability to Make a Plan and Stick To It.

3) How can you use your answers from question #2 to increase your level of intentional decision making?

4) How can this help you change your mind-set?

5) Write one goal related to changing your mind-set in the aspect of goal setting.

CHOOSE YOUR
CIRCLE WISELY

Chapter **9**

CHOOSE YOUR CIRCLE WISELY

E mbarking on the path to success often means out-
growing familiar faces and places. It's not easy to
accept, but not everyone will celebrate your evolution. As you grow, your values, habits, and daily routines
will begin to shift. That change isn't random it's the natural
result of seeing the world through a new lens. The things
that once thrilled you may now feel empty. Activities that
once filled your days may start to feel like distractions. In
truth, your entire way of living will begin to transform.

One key difference between those who grow and those
who stay stuck is this: understanding the power of choice.
Most people overlook this truth. But you won't be one of
them. You'll be among the few who realize that the gap
between where you are and where you want to be is bridged
by the decisions you make nothing more, nothing less.

To some, this may sound overly simplistic. But don't underestimate it. Making a choice is one of the most powerful acts you can take. Decide what you want. Craft a practical plan to achieve it. Write it down. Then follow through consistently and intentionally until you reach your goal.

When your decisions are intentional and backed by action, your mindset begins to shift. And as your thoughts change, so will your environment. The world around you will have no choice but to adjust to the new you.

That "world" isn't just some abstract concept. It's the people you interact with, the places you visit, and the things that engage your five senses. Those senses feed your conscious mind the part of you that thinks, plans, and reasons. But beneath that lies a deeper, quieter force: your subconscious mind. It works in the background, shaping your reality without any conscious effort.

The subconscious mind can be influenced—often without you even realizing it. Whatever consistently dominates your conscious thoughts will eventually become impressed upon your subconscious. This is crucial to understand because once something is embedded in your subconscious mind, you will begin to act on it automatically, without deliberate thought.

The subconscious operates effortlessly and continuously it never sleeps. It runs 24 hours a day, even when you're asleep. That's why it's vital to be intentional about who you surround yourself with.

Why is this important?

Because your closest associates through their words, behaviors, and beliefs will inevitably influence your subconscious mind. Whether you're aware of it or not, this influence can shape your actions, decisions, and even your future. This psychological truth is what gives weight to the saying, "Birds of a feather flock together."

Think about it. How similar are your lifestyle, mindset, and habits to those of your closest friends? Chances are, if two or more of your friends are wealthy, you're either financially stable yourself or on the path to becoming so. This shared trajectory is no coincidence. It results from a phenomenon I call co-occurring success, which stems from two forces:

1. Emulation
2. The Reticular Activating System (R.A.S.)

Emulation is our innate drive to match or surpass the people around us. It's human nature to mirror those we admire or associate closely with.

The Reticular Activating System, on the other hand, is more intricate. This is the mental filter that, once something is deemed important by your subconscious, directs your attention to anything related to it. In other words, once your subconscious identifies something as a priority, your R.A.S. starts noticing and highlighting opportunities, tools, people, and resources connected to that goal.

Together, emulation and the R.A.S. shape what your mind sees as valuable, helping you locate what you need to pursue and ultimately achieve that goal.

For example, have you ever bought a car, and once you bought it, you started noticing the same kind of car everywhere? If so, you have experienced the intriguing power of the R.A.S. To simplify all of this, let me put it this way: If you have five friends who are millionaires, it is highly likely that you will become the sixth, because, you will begin to speak, behave, and think in the manner that they do. Jim Rohn put it beautifully when he said, "You are the average of the top 5 people you spend the most time with." Read the foregoing sentence again, and realize that this is great news for you.

How so, you ask?

Because it means that if you will simply change the type of people you associate with, you will inevitably change your life. This is the reason it is of the utmost importance that you *Choose Your Circle Wisely.*

Don't get it twisted; simply having millionaire friends won't make you a millionaire. You don't magically become successful; you must put in work. You have to become what they are, and assimilate their way of thinking.

Think about it for a second, why would a millionaire allow you to hang around them? You must exhibit qualities that they deem valuable. Why? Because, the key to becoming wealthy, or successful, is not a matter of how much labor you do, it is a matter of how much value you add to others.

It's imperative that you understand that who you associate with will have an affect your life. The only question is will it be positively or negatively. This choice is yours.

This chapter is one of, if not the most, important chapters in this book. You cannot be passive about anything in your life.

You must live with intentionality.

Every choice you make has a consequence, be it good or bad. The same way you make a choice about every *thing* in your life, you must also make choices about every *person* you allow in your life. With this in mind allow me to lend you this note of advice again:

> *Any person whose life values strongly oppose*
> *yours should not be in your life.*

The more certain you are about who you are, what you require out of life, and what you are willing to do to get it, the easier it will be to see in others the qualities that harmonize with your intentions.

UNDERSTAND YOU, SO YOU
CAN UNDERSTAND THEM

It's a well-established truth: two minds are better than one. Rarely does anyone achieve significant success entirely on their own. Behind every major accomplishment, you'll almost always find at least one other person who contributed to that journey. So here's a phrase worth writing down and keeping front and center not just committing to memory, but living by:

Your team is everything.

But not just any team will do. Your team must be thoughtfully and intentionally assembled. Surround yourself with people who complement your strengths those who excel in areas where you might struggle. Seek individuals who can generate ideas you'd never think of and push boundaries you might hesitate to cross. A great team brings balance not just to your business, but to your life as a whole.

Napoleon Hill, in his timeless classic *Think and Grow Rich*, refers to this kind of team as a Mastermind group. These are the people you lean on and who, in turn, lean on you. Mutual trust, shared vision, and aligned purpose are the foundation of such a group. Whether you're building a business or pursuing any goal that demands excellence, a strong, supportive team is non-negotiable.

Be loyal to your team. Challenge them to grow. Reward them when they rise to the occasion. And most importantly, be self-aware when choosing your team. You must intentionally seek out individuals who possess the qualities you lack.

But here's the catch: in order to identify what you need in others, you first need to understand yourself.

This section is designed to help you do just that. Because the better you know yourself, the better you'll be at recognizing who you need around you. So let's begin with a simple, yet revealing question:

What type of thinker are you?

To help you answer that, I've developed a self-assessment. While there are many personality tests and thinking-style models out there, the one you'll encounter here is unique to this book. I call it the **Finesse Test.**

Finesse is defined as: refinement or delicacy of workmanship, the skillful handling of a situation to bring about, direct or manage by adroit maneuvering.

The Finesse Test, is a self-assessment designed to help you understand what type of thinker you are, and how best to utilize your natural abilities to achieve the highest levels of workmanship you can.

The Finesse Test will help you find out what kind of thinker you are, and how to use this knowledge to do anything successfully, including owning your own business.

In today's society the word finesse has taken a bad wrap, because it is often used as a form of slang. A lot of the time people use it as a way to say that one person tricked another out of something, but in its purest form, it means skillfulness. Ok, now that we got that out of the way, let's specify how we are going to change the narrative on finesse.

After you take the *Finesse Test*, and learn your *Finesse Type*, I am going to help you learn how to *Refine Your Finesse*, by actively choosing what type of people you associate with.

Before we begin, note that there are four types of thinkers:

*Type A
*Type B
*Type C
*Type D

Let's begin by describing how each Finesse Type likes to lead:

LEADERSHIP STYLES

Type A: This type of leader:

- Runs well structured meetings
- Make good logistics experts
- Gets the job done regardless of what happens
- Provides a good stabilizing force
- Understands the importance and value of ceremony

Type B: This type of leader:

- Quickly diagnose problems
- Are natural fun lovers
- Pushes teams to new limits
- Work best under pressure
- Recognizes opportunity where others don't

Type C: This Type of leader:

- Understands the balancing of process with outcomes
- Brings inspiration and enthusiasm
- Seeks group participation
- Creates great "open" environments
- Great at developing teams

Type D: This type of leader:

- Excellent team planner
- Are "Big Picture" people (they see the big picture)
- Are critical thinkers
- Efficient
- Seeks to challenge the status quo

So, now that we understand how each Finesse Type leads, and how their leadership contributes to the **team**, let's learn what type of **individuals** they are. This part is important because, when building a business, or working towards a definite goal you need to know your people's leadership style and personality type in order to put them in the areas where they are good and you are not. (Note: Each Finesse type has its own unique personality traits, though some traits may overlap.)

PERSONALITY TRAITS

Type A: These are the people who rely on facts. They use facts and details to make their decision. These types of people must feel like they "belong," and they thrive off of earning this place of belonging by being useful in many ways, such as:

- Fulfilling responsibilities
- Being of Service
- Giving to others instead of receiving from them

Key fact: They expect those around them to be accountable and hardworking.

Type B: These are the people also rely heavily on facts, but they tend to live "in the moment," and need the autonomy to act, and make decisions.

Key fact: They tend to be impulsive, free-spirited, and values freedom and autonomy above all else.

Type C: These are the people who trust and rely on their intuition. They make decisions based on personal values rather than facts. They like to be seen as "authentic." Honesty, to them, is expecting the same of themselves as they expect of others.

Key fact: Their life and work must have meaning.

Type D: These are the people who are logical and competent. They value and trust their intuition, but do not necessarily rely on it. They are always searching for truth and knowledge.

Key fact: These people look to obtain abilities and skills.

Now that we know more about the personality of each Finesse Type, let's look at the strengths and characteristics of each type.

STEGNTHS & CHARACTERISTICS

Type A:

- Great Planners
- Detail Oriented
- Organized
- Rule Followers
- Structured
- Punctual
- Believes in policies.

These people believe in being prepared. They are loyal, dependable, trustworthy, and decisive.

Key strengths: These are the people you can turn to when you need to establish policies, need a strong backbone for the organization, or need someone who have a strong work ethic and pays attention to detail.

Type B:

- Impulsive
- Accepts Challenges
- Pushes Boundaries
- Energetic
- Self-confident
- Seeks out change

These people believe in going full steam ahead, provides spontaneity, loves variety and performs well.

Key strengths: These are the people you can count on in crisis situations, when you need problems dealt with quickly, or you need leadership.

Type C:

- Optimistic
- Passionate
- People Oriented
- Enthusiastic
- Imaginative
- Cooperative

These people believe in the value of relationships, and are authentic and unique. They lead by democracy, understand the importance of organization and sees potential in other people.

Key strengths: These are the types you can turn to when you need a mentor, someone who trains well, need creative ideas, or simply need understanding. These people are catalysts.

Type D:

- Intellectual
- Independent
- Problem Solver
- Perfectionists
- Analytical
- Calm & Collected

These people believe in the power of knowledge, they provide clarity, they are critical thinkers, and they are comfortable with rapid change.

Key strengths: These are the types you can turn to when you need objective decision making, someone with tenacity, information and analytical skills. These people usually have extensive technological information.

Ok, now that we know the leadership style, personality traits, and key strengths of each Finesse Type, let's find out what type you are!

Instructions:

1) View the chart and answer the questions going from left to right. (as you would read the words in a book)
2) Once you have answered all the questions on one line, move down to the next line and repeat.
3) Repeat this process until all questions (statements) are completed.

FINESSE TEST

Below are groups of words in rows. Score each group of words (going across), using the following scale:

Rate each statement in accordance with how close to your personality the statement:

- **Least like you: 1**
- **A little like you: 2**
- **Like you: 3**
- **Highly like you: 4**

Active Opportunistic Spontaneous	Parental Traditional Responsible	Authentic Harmonious Compassion	Versatile Inventive Competent
Competitive Impetuous Impactful	Practical Sensible Dependable	Unique Empathetic Communicative	Curious Conceptual Knowledgeable
Realistic Open-minded Adventuresome	Loyal Conservative Organized	Devoted Warm Poetic	Theoretical Seeking Ingenious
Daring Impulsive Fun	Concerned Procedural Cooperative	Tender Inspirational Dramatic	Determined Complex Composed
Exciting Courageous Skillful	Ordered Conventional Caring	Vivacious Affectionate Sympathetic	Philosophical Principled Rational
TOTAL:	TOTAL:	TOTAL:	TOTAL:
Column A	Column B	Column C	Column D

FINESSE TEST

Ok, that was easy enough, right? Now that you have finished scoring each group of statements, here is how you find out what *Finesse Type* you have:

RESULTS:

Once you are finished, tally up your total score in each column going from top to bottom. Once you have totaled up your score in each column, look at the column that you have the highest total score in. This is your Finesse Type. Below is a list of the columns that match the corresponding Finesse Type:

Column A: Finesse Type B

Column B: Finesse Type A

Column C: Finesse Type C

Column D: Finesse Type D

Note: Some people may have two columns with the same high score, this is not a bad thing it only means that you have a mixture of two Finesse Types. (hybrid Finesse)

REFINE YOUR FINESSE

Now that you've identified your own Finesse Type, encourage your team members to take the assessment as well. Understanding each person's Finesse Type allows you to strategically structure your organization's leadership for maximum growth and efficiency. This is what it means to refine your Finesse: by understanding how your team thinks, you can position each individual where they can contribute the most value.

For example, if you want your organization to have a strong backbone, operate in a well-organized manner, and be governed by clear policies and rules, you'll need a Type A individual at the helm. On the other hand, if you envision a company that is cooperative, people-oriented, and fosters an open, inclusive environment, a Type C leader would be the best fit.

You can even take this concept further.

Perhaps your goal is to build a multifaceted organization one where people of all types can work harmoniously in a structured yet people-centered environment, guided by fair and transparent policies. In this case, your CEO could be a Type A personality, while your company President is a Type C. The combinations are endless.

The Finesse Test can be applied to structure any group setting, whether it's a business, a project team, or any collective effort where people are working toward a shared goal.

There is no single "right" way to apply it. What matters most is aligning your structure with your vision.

Let the examples above serve as a guide and spark ideas for how to use the Finesse Test to enhance your organization. Remember, they are just possibilities not rules. Choose the direction you want your organization to go, and use the Finesse Test to help you place the right people in the right roles to bring that vision to life.

IT'S UP TO YOU

It is my dearest hope that this chapter can be both an enlightenment, and a tool that you can use to bring your goals closer to fruition. The process of actively choosing the people who you allow to be a part of your life is of vital importance. I cannot provide all the knowledge of the Great Thinkers centuries past in this one book, but I can leave you with key information that is good, true, and has worked, without fail, since history has been recorded. One of those key pieces of information is this:

Dreams and plans are worthless without action.

Act now and succeed.

Or, procrastinate and fail.

It's up to you.

Knowledge is infinite. That means there's no limit to what you can learn. So if you THINK you're the smartest person in the room, then you have been in that room, and around the same people for too long. You must always stay open and receptive to new information via friends, family, coaches, elders, and experiences.

– *Charlamagne Tha God*

INTENTIONAL WORK

1) What key points from the chapter resonated with you?

2) Name three ways you can use this to improve your ability to Choose Your Circle Wisely.

3) How can you use your answers from question #2 to increase your level of intentional decision making?

4) How can this help you change your mind-set?

5) Write one goal related to changing your mind-set in the aspect of associating the right people.

GOD'S PLAN (HARMONY)

Chapter 10

GOD'S PLAN (HARMONY)

Although different religious traditions may use various names to describe the universal force behind all of existence, one truth remains constant: there is an invisible source from which everything originates and by which all life is sustained. Some call it "Nature," others refer to it as "The Universe." Regardless of the label, this infinite power exists and it works for the good of all life. It operates beyond race, creed, background, or ethnicity, offering its presence to every human being equally.

As for me, I identify with the Christian faith, and so I choose to call this power God. From this point forward, I'll refer to the source as such. I also believe that God came to us in human form as Jesus Christ and that Jesus left us with life-changing principles for living a joyful, meaningful, and spiritually fulfilled life.

One of the most profound of these principles is this: true success begins with doing good to others. Jesus emphasized this truth time and again. In Luke 6:31 (NLT), He tells us, "Do to others as you would like them to do to you." That wasn't just a moral suggestion; it was a key to living a life filled with more than material wealth or worldly accomplishments. Jesus was showing us the way to a life enriched with love, inner peace, and lasting joy all of which are essential to experiencing true success.

Now, some might challenge this idea by pointing to the apparent success of those who don't live by such principles those who mistreat others and still rise to power or wealth. But I would argue that these individuals only appear to succeed. If we could peer beyond the surface, I believe we would often find lives filled with anxiety, conflict, emptiness, and unrest.

Yes, they may have money, cars, clothes, and all the other things that people usually measure success by, but do they have peace? Do they have love? These are the things true success is measured by, because true success is peaceful. Remember this:

> God will never allow you to gain something without giving something of equal or exceeding value in return.

If you take the time to observe nature, you'll notice a powerful principle at work: everything that gains does so by giving. This is why I firmly believe that God will never allow you to truly gain something without giving something of equal or greater value in return.

Consider those who acquire wealth through illicit means without offering any real value in exchange. More often than not, they eventually lose everything, whether it's their freedom, their wealth, or both. A classic example is the neighborhood drug dealer. It's not that he's doomed simply because he's "bad," but because he's receiving money without giving genuine value. Contrary to popular belief, drugs are not a value-adding commodity.

They destroy lives rather than build them.

Ill-gotten wealth comes at a high price paid not by the one receiving it, but by those from whom it is taken. It may cost someone their health, their freedom, their property, or even their life. While I acknowledge that some socioeconomic situations can leave people feeling cornered into bad decisions, the truth remains: taking without giving violates the natural and divine order of how the universe is meant to operate.

The good news is that you don't have to take from others in order to succeed. This book has given you countless examples and strategies for achieving your dreams ethically and sustainably. If you apply these principles consistently and intentionally, there's no doubt you will succeed.

But there's one more thing you must do: believe.

In Mark 9:23 (NLT), Jesus said to the father of a demon-possessed boy, "What do you mean, 'If I can'?" Then He added, "Anything is possible if a person believes."

In that moment, Jesus revealed the key to success not just for that desperate father, but for all of us.

Even if your goal isn't healing like his was, the principle still applies. Whatever you're striving for whether it's peace, success, or a fulfilled life it starts with belief.

You have to believe it's possible.

Be advised, there is no such reality as something for nothing. Everything in nature was created to co-exist in harmony and help the entire ecosystem sustain. All life forms have to do their individual part to ensure that the whole of life itself continues to exist. Take, for instance, the relationship between humans and trees, or plants and bees.

Through this process of one life form helping another, life continually searches out ways to exist on higher levels. Scientists call it evolution; I call it God's Plan:

> *Everything in nature works together in harmony to continue existing and expressing itself on higher planes.*

This is a universal law of nature, and as such, this law must also apply to your life in order for you to achieve success.

THERE IS NO I IN TEAM, BUT THERE IS A U IN US

It is well known that the Holy Bible is considered the written Word of God, scribed by various individuals inspired by the Holy Spirit. One such person was Paul. In the New Testament, in his letter to the church in Rome, Paul writes:

> "May God, who gives this patience and encouragement, help you live in complete harmony with each other, as is fitting for followers of Christ." Romans 15:5 (NLT)

My intention in sharing this scripture is not to debate whether one should be a follower of Christ. Every person must make their own choice regarding matters of faith. Rather, my goal is to highlight the significance of harmony. If we believe the Bible to be God's Word, then it follows that God saw harmony as so vital that He inspired Paul to write about it.

That, to me, is something we cannot afford to overlook.

Harmony can be defined as the alignment of parts with one another and with the whole. It fosters cooperation among people which is crucial, because achieving your dreams will require the support and cooperation of others. I encourage you to actively seek ways to build harmonious relationships in your life, where everyone involved feels genuinely valued.

This is especially true when it comes to the team of individuals who assist you in reaching your goals.

Anyone willing to help you succeed should feel deeply appreciated whether they are business partners, employees, co-workers, friends, family members, or romantic partners.

In a truly harmonious relationship, all parties give and receive. No one should ever feel expected to continually give without also receiving. The same principle applies to you: if you find yourself in a relationship where you consistently give but do not receive, that relationship is not operating in harmony. It must either be mended or ended.

In Mark 12:31 *(The Holy Bible NLT version)*, Jesus implores us to, "love your neighbor as yourself." The wisdom in this advice can be easily discovered with the asking of one question: How would you feel if someone used your talent, or intellectual property to gain monetary value, and then split none of the proceeds with you? Without even hearing your reply, I know you would feel cheated. Appropriately, it should always be your goal as a leader to never cause those who are a part of your team to feel this way.

If you live by Jesus' tenets you know you should never do to another person anything that you would not want someone to do to you. The average person would be upset about a situation such as the one described earlier. To illustrate how Jesus teaches us to avoid these types of disharmonious situations I turn again to Luke 6:31 *(The Holy Bible NLT version)*, He said "Do unto others as you would have them do unto you". In both of these scriptures the truths held in them teach the same lesson, but in order for them to work to your benefit, you have to imbue them into your life, your team, and your business.

Always look to do good unto others, and good will come to you.

HARMONY IS HONEST

A business is built on many things capital, products, technology but above all, it is built on people. A company is nothing without the individuals who help run it day in and day out. Your team is everything. Be honest with them. Let them know where you are, where you're headed, and how you plan to get there.

Be equally transparent about your limitations. You might be surprised at how far your team will go to support you when they understand what you need and feel genuinely appreciated.

Employees are people, not just roles. They have families, dreams, and aspirations of their own so treat them accordingly. People who feel like valued members of an organization, rather than just cogs in the machine, tend to work harder and more efficiently. This is known as buy-in.

There are several ways to help your team see that their success is tied to yours. Profit-sharing programs, performance incentives, and bonuses are just a few examples.

When you create an environment where your employees win when you win, you foster a culture of harmony within your organization.

And in a harmonious environment, everything thrives.

Remember this: be honest, do good, and show genuine care for others. When you do, harmony will become a natural part of your life and with it, the ability to achieve beyond your wildest dreams.

You only deserve what you earn.

– Atu Campbell

INTENTIONAL WORK

1) What key points from the chapter resonated with you?

2) Name three ways you can use this to improve your ability to bring Harmony to the world around you.

3) How can you use your answers from question #2 to increase your level of intentional decision making?

4) How can this help you change your mind-set?

5) Write one goal related to changing your mind-set in the aspect of living harmoniously.

CONSIDER
THE COST

Chapter *11*

CONSIDER THE COST

I n the previous chapters of this book, we've explored how to pursue your dreams, overcome self-doubt, silence outside opinions, and create harmony in your life. But this chapter is different. This is my final exhortation a heartfelt plea for you to cut off all negative influences from your life. Why? Because negativity isn't just emotionally draining; it has real, measurable impacts on your mental and physical health.

This chapter focuses on the concept of social stress and the damage it can cause, not just in how you think and feel, but in how your body functions.

Social stress has tangible, physiological effects that can quietly erode your quality of life. It activates the sympathetic nervous system, which is housed in the thoracic region of the spinal cord. This system counters the calming effects of the parasympathetic nervous system, ramping up your heart rate, constricting blood vessels, and suppressing digestion in response to perceived threats.

In moderation, stress can be useful even healthy serving as a motivator or warning signal. But chronic stress is a different story. Long-term elevation of cortisol, the body's primary stress hormone, has been linked to a wide array of health issues: fatigue, digestive problems, weakened immunity, anxiety, and even chronic disease.

Thanks to Neuroendocrinology, the study of how the brain and hormones interact, we now understand more about how social dynamics contribute to stress. One study (Dickerson, Mycek, & Zaldivar, 2008) asked undergraduate students to deliver a speech either alone or in front of two observers. When students performed in front of others, their cortisol levels spiked significantly. The takeaway? Simply being judged by others can trigger a biological stress response, comparable to that caused by more obvious, chronic stressors.

Why does this happen?

Because social stress is hardwired into us. In prehistoric times, being rejected by your tribe often meant death. You needed the group to survive. Acceptance was safety. Rejection could be fatal. That primal wiring still exists today even though the world around us has changed drastically.

In the modern era, our "tribes" might be friends, coworkers, online communities, or family members. And although physical survival no longer depends on social inclusion, our bodies still respond to social rejection as if it's a threat to our lives. This outdated biological response leads to unhealthy behaviors and coping mechanisms that are counterproductive in the context of modern living.

Some of the most common examples include:

- Perfectionism – driven by the fear of judgment and rejection
- People-pleasing – rooted in the desire to stay in favor with others
- Comparison – fueled by the need to measure up and "belong"

These tendencies, while once protective, are now barriers to peace, authenticity, and progress.

PERFECTIONISM

Perfectionism is a Trap, Here's Why You Should Let It Go

Perfectionism is the constant need to always do the "right" thing. People who struggle with perfectionism often stress over the perceived correctness of their actions. They obsess over details like what to wear, how they look to others, or whether they're saying the right things.

The tragic truth? Perfectionists forget a fundamental reality: no one is perfect. Their relentless pursuit of flawlessness is ultimately futile. Trying to appear perfect in the eyes of others becomes a never-ending cycle of disappointment and emotional exhaustion. No matter what you do, someone will always find fault with it. So why bother trying to meet an impossible standard?

Here's the good news: you don't need to be perfect because your worth and survival are not dependent on anyone's approval. In today's world, you have the freedom to choose who gets access to your energy and presence. You can live a full, meaningful life surrounded by people who value and appreciate you for who you are, not who you're pretending to be.

Stop subjecting yourself to the chronic stress of trying to be everything to everyone. It's not only unnecessary it's harmful to your well-being. Release the burden of perfection and embrace authenticity instead. That's where real peace lives.

PEOPLE-PLEASING

Stop People-Pleasing Before It Stops You

People-pleasing is the constant, exhausting worry of not wanting to upset or offend anyone. At its core, it's a deep vulnerability one that others can often sense and, sadly, exploit. Some individuals will take advantage of a people-pleaser's psychological need for approval, manipulating them for personal gain.

Those caught in this trap try desperately to please everyone, only to end up in situations they never wanted to be in emotionally drained, misused, and far from their true path.

The most heartbreaking part? People-pleasing often leads to the complete abandonment of self-preservation. That's the real danger. When the need to make others happy outweighs your own safety, well-being, and purpose, you put your entire life at risk. And some literally have lost their lives because of it. That's how powerful this silent struggle can be.

At the root of people-pleasing is a false belief: that making everyone else happy will result in love, validation, and belonging. But here's the truth it never does. People-pleasers pour enormous time and energy into meeting everyone's expectations, only to find that satisfaction never comes.

Why? Because it's impossible to please everyone.

Instead of chasing unattainable approval, that energy would be far better spent building your self-confidence, learning to stand in your own truth without needing a crowd to cheer you on.

Let me remind you of something crucial: we are no longer living in prehistoric times. Your survival no longer depends on being accepted by a tribe. You don't need universal approval to thrive.

If you've recognized yourself in these words, don't panic, I've been there too. And I'm here to tell you: you can break free. The first step is a commitment to change. You can win this battle by learning to truly love yourself. Embrace your uniqueness that's your superpower. Use positive self-talk, surround yourself with affirming influences, and cut out the voices that sow doubt.

Here's the bottom line: it doesn't matter what everyone else thinks. Their acceptance doesn't determine your future. They don't hold the keys to your success, your peace, or your purpose. You do.

So spend your life pleasing the one person who truly matters you. Pursue your dreams. Live boldly. And never forget: self-love isn't selfish it's survival.

COMPARISON

Comparing ourselves to others is so common that we often accept it as normal but that doesn't make it healthy. Many people who fall into this habit assume, often mistakenly, that everyone else is more confident, more successful, or more put together. This perception fuels a cycle of self-doubt that quietly erodes self-esteem.

Comparison takes many forms, but for the purposes of this book, I want to focus on two of the most damaging: Upward Comparison and Downward Comparison.

Upward Comparison occurs when we look at someone we perceive to be more accomplished, attractive, or successful and feel inferior as a result. This can trigger feelings of envy, inadequacy, or self-judgment. In small doses and with the right mindset, upward comparison can be motivating it might inspire you to grow or aim higher. However, it becomes harmful when it leads to negative self-talk or a distorted sense of your own worth. When admiration turns into self-criticism, comparison becomes a trap rather than a tool.

On the other hand, Downward Comparison happens when someone looks down on another person in order to feel better about themselves. This often manifests as silent judgment or overt criticism. At its core, downward comparison is a form of avoidance it helps people ignore their own issues by focusing on someone else's flaws. But make no mistake: this mindset is rooted in denial and insecurity. If you need to tear others down to lift yourself up, you're standing on shaky ground.

We've all been guilty of this at some point. But the goal is to become aware of it and stop it in its tracks. If you catch yourself engaging in downward comparison, shift the thought immediately. Replace judgment with compassion and criticism with gratitude.

Let me give you an example. Suppose you see someone who is overweight and your first reaction is, "I would never want to look like that." Instead of lingering in that judgmental space, reframe your thinking. Try something like, "I'm grateful for my health, and I hope that person finds the strength to improve theirs if they choose to." It's not about pity; it's about replacing negativity with empathy and redirecting your focus inward.

At the end of the day, comparison whether upward or downward is a distraction from your own journey. You don't need to measure yourself against anyone else, because there's no one else exactly like you. Your path is your own. Walk it with confidence.

TAKEAWAYS

Social stress can be equally harmful. It can cause both mental and physical consequences, such as impaired parasympathetic function and long-term anxiety. But here's the empowering part you don't have to let it ruin your well-being. You can choose not to give in to the pressure of outside opinions. When you feel the weight of social stress, that's not your signal to retreat. It's your opportunity to grow. Growth happens when you learn to be comfortable being uncomfortable. When you start noticing that certain relationships are shifting, or people who once sought your company no longer do, that's often a sign you're on the right path, your own path.

Social stress is a common part of everyday life. Most people experience it, even if they never show it. But here's the thing you are not average. You cannot afford to let social stress derail your plans, your goals, or your dreams. That's why it's essential to apply the tools and strategies in this book to strengthen your self-confidence and protect it fiercely.

Here are few questions that you can ask yourself to get to the source of what causes you to experience social stress:

1) What triggers negative social thoughts most often?
2) Why do I fear what people will think of me?
3) When did I first realize this fear?
4) What methods can I use from *Intentionally You* to gain control over this fear?

Use the answers to these questions to help yourself overcome the ill of social stress. Refuse to let it be an obstruction to your path to success, because you owe it to yourself to succeed. My final exhortation is to be encouraged. You must put in the work to transcend the opinions of others. Through persistent effort you can develop the self-confidence to overcome the fear of rejection which, I believe, is the root cause of social stress. No person on this earth is worth you stressing over what they think so much that your health is negatively affected.

It is your life, your breath, and your body.

The only person whose opinion matters is yours.

Remember, the only person who can stop you from overcoming doubt, silencing outside opinions, and accomplishing your dreams is you!

INTENTIONAL WORK

1) What key points from the chapter resonated with you?

2) Name three ways you can use this to improve your ability to Consider the Cost.

3) How can you use your answers from question #2 to increase your level of intentional decision making?

4) How can this help you change your mind-set?

5) Write one goal related to changing your mind-set in the aspect of defeating social stress.

INTENTIONALLY YOU

Chapter *12*

INTENTIONALLY YOU

This chapter is different. It's less of a traditional chapter and more of a love letter to the future you. It's my way of giving you your flowers now. I'm congratulating you ahead of time, because I believe in you. I don't need to wait to witness the beautiful existence your life becomes, because I already know what God placed inside of you.

I wish I could fully express the depth of your power. Words fall short. But know this: you carry within you an immeasurable strength, a light capable of transforming not only your life but the lives of others. And so, I encourage you: be a responsible steward of your power. Use it for good. Share your gifts to uplift the world. Help when you can. Encourage others when the opportunity arises. And know this—when your intentions are rooted in love and service, you cannot fail.

Without further ado, here is my letter to the new you...

Dear Future You,

Be proud of yourself in this moment. You took your life into your own hands and made the bold decision to live with intention. You chose to rise. You claimed your place in the world not by chance, but by choice. Every step you took was deliberate. Every decision was aligned with your purpose. You understood that nothing in life is random; each choice either brings you closer to or pulls you further from your destiny. And so, you chose the road less traveled. You ran toward your calling.

Since the beginning, you've been a seeker an unshakable leader on a lifelong quest to learn, grow, and embody your vision. You've always seen yourself doing what others might call impossible. How do I know this about you, even though we've never met? Because you are here, right now, reading this letter. That tells me everything.

You're reading this because you value education, self-mastery, and growth. You understand that success is more than status or credentials, it's the power to transform your world and lift up others with you. And you've done exactly that.

Fulfilling your dream was never just a fantasy it was a necessity. You knew you deserved it. You had the confidence to go after it, no matter how many times life knocked you down. Yes, you've tried before. You've tasted the dream, then watched it slip through your fingers. But this time... you finished what you started.

This time, you changed your life.

You fought through the setbacks. You endured the disappointments. And you rose just like a phoenix from the ashes. You didn't let failure define you. You turned it into fuel. You walked through fire and emerged refined, renewed, and whole. Now, you are exactly who you were always meant to be.

Confident.
Strong.
Free.
And most of all...

Intentionally You.

INTENTIONAL WORK

1) What key points from the letter resonated with you?

2) Name three ways you can identify with the letter.

3) How can you use the letter as encouragement?

4) How can this help you change your mind-set?

5) Write one goal related to changing your mind-set in the aspect of living Intentionally.

Write down what you became on your journey to self-mastery:

YOU BELIEVED IN YOUR VISION. NOW YOU CAN LOOK IN THE MIRROR AND TELL YOURSELF:

I AM A _____.

SIMPLY BECAUSE I CHOSE TO LIVE WITH INTENTION.

THANK YOU

Thanks,

Thank you first and foremost to my Lord and Savior, Jesus Christ. Also, to everyone who took the time to read this book, I pray it has been blessing to your life. Thank you to my family, to everyone who stood beside me all this time. Through the ups and downs, you were down for me. I would have never imagined that my life would take this path, but I never gave up and neither did you. To Myya, thank you for always being there for me, and bearing my firstborn son, for this I am forever indebted to you. To Donald, my day one. We have seen a lot together homie, thank you for being my best friend, and always looking out for me even when everyone else left me for dead you didn't, and if I have never told you, brother I love you and value our friendship immensely. To mom, dad, Aunt Lee, and Uncle Monroe you created me, you raised me to be the man I am, thank you for never leaving my side. To Tericka, thank you for being a true friend, and blessing me with my babies Caiden and Niyah

Pooh, for giving me them, you will always hold a special place in my life. To Rukiya, my sister, my best friend, I love you boo. You are the definition of a strong black woman. I value you immensely and I love you deeply, I would give my life for you big sis. Anything I have, you have. All that is mine is yours... I love you sis. To Debbie and Wookie, I love you both deeply. My big sis Debbie, you hold a special place in my heart, I will never forget the days when you raised me like I was your own. I love you big sis anything you need, if I don't have it, I will get it... I love you big sis. To my niece, Aaliyaha, I love you baby. I know I haven't always been the best uncle, but I want you to know I would lay down my life for you, I love you. Last, but not least, my babies Carson, Caiden, Aniyah, and Jun. I love you guys more than I can explain. I am so proud of each one of you. Though I haven't been the perfect father, I want you to know that I love you with a perfect love. Everyday of my life I work on improving myself for you guys, and building a legacy of generational wealth for you to inherit. To my cousins Tae, Lil E, Duke, and Dredd, I love you like my brothers and I appreciate you for always holding me down. I could always depend on you guys and I hope you know you can always depend on me as well. To all those who I didn't name specifically, charge it to my head and not my heart. I want you to know that I thank God for you, I love you and appreciate you. Thank you

Love,
Atu Olatunji Campbell

NOTES

Chapter Two: "Education is more than school; education is knowledge." and "Education is important, but once you've got the education, it's got to be balanced with expression and excellence."

Thomas, Eric. *You Owe You: Ignite Your Power, Your Purpose, and Your Why*. New York: Penguin Random House 2022.

Chapter Two: "For my people lending their strength to the years, to the gone years, and the new years and the maybe years, washing, ironing, cooking, scrubbing, sewing, mending, hoeing, plowing, digging, planting, pruning, dragging along never reaping, never knowing and never understanding."

Walker, Margaret. *For My People*. August 2025. http://www.poettryfoundation.ore/poetrymagazine/poems/21850/for-my-people.

Chapter Two: "Man is a thinking center, and can originate thoughts. All the forms that man fashions with his hands must first exist in his thoughts. Man cannot shape a thing until he has thought the thing."

Wattles, Wallace D. *The Science of Getting Rich: The proven mental program to a life of wealth*. New York: J.P. Tarcher/Penguin 2007.

Chapter Two: "Achievement Loop." and "In my coaching, I've observed this loop in action. When individuals embrace confidence, they're more likely to set ambitious goals, embrace challenges, and persevere in the face of setbacks." and "Forward momentum often leads to tangible results, which further strengthens their belief in themselves."

Ross, Sana. *The Science of Confidence: Why Self-Belief is Linked to Achievements*. May 12, 2025. http://www.sanaross.com/the -neuroscience-of-achieving-more/the-science-of-confidence-why-self-belief-is-linked-to-achievements#.

Chapter Four: "Unique Ability®" and "1) It is a superior ability that you have.. 2) You love doing it… 3) It is energizing... 4) You keep getting better…"

Sullivan, Dan. *Discover Your Natural Strengths: Finding Your Unique Ability*. August 2025. http://www.roughnotes. com/mmagazine/2012/august2012/2012_08p076.htm

Chapter Four: "Most individuals are not able to identify their Unique Ability, let alone concentrate on it, because they are trapped by childhood training. We learn at a young age that the secret to success in life is working on our weaknesses. Unfortunately this focus on weaknesses creates a sense of inadequacy, failure and guilt."

Addis, Scott. Discover Your Natural Strengths: Finding Your Unique Ability. August 2025. http://www.roughnotes.com/mmagazine/2012/august2012/2012_08p076.htm

Chapter Seven: "Freedom is never given; it's won."

Randolph, Philip A. Hall of Honor Inductee. August 2025. http://www.dol.gov/general/about/hallofhonor/1989_randolph.

Chapter Seven: "The dedication to work hard is necessary for personal growth and ultimately to achieve our definition of success. Beyond the tangible rewards, such dedication plays a pivotal role in fostering self-awareness and achieving clarity of vision."

Branson, Creed. The Power of Dedication: A Path to Success, Self-Awareness, and Clarity of Vision. January 2024. http://www.creedbranson.com/the-power-of-dedication/

Chapter Nine: "Mastermind group"

Hill, Napoleon. Think *and Grow Rich: The Landmark Bestseller-Now Revised And Updated For The 21st Century.* New York: Penguin 2005.

Chapter Nine: "You are the average of the top 5 people you spend the most time with."

Rohn, Jim. Show Me Your Friends and I'll Show You Your Future-lead you first. March 2025. http://www.leadyoufirst.com/relationships-shape-your-life/.

Chapter Eleven: The study of Neuroendocrinology information was received from this source. "One study asked undergraduates to deliver a speech..."

(Dickerson, Mycek, & Zaldivar, 2008)

ABOUT THE AUTHOR

Atu Campbell is a driven entrepreneur, and the cofounder of several successful ventures, including Legacy Journey Group LLC, and A&R Business Corp. A native of Memphis, Tennessee, Atu's journey is one of transformation, resilience, and purpose.

Due to his unique experience of being a justice impacted individual, Atu made the decision to help others realize that setbacks don't determine your potential. He made the life-changing decision to shift his mindset, pursue a path of personal growth and business success, and encourage others that they can do the same.

During his time inside, he earned an Associate Degree in Business Administration, co-founded two companies, earned his license as a Certified Peer Recovery Specialist, and is currently continuing his education working toward his Bachelor's degree with the overall goal of one day attaining his Ph.D.

Atu's experiences have fueled his passion for empowering others to break barriers, redefine their futures, and create lasting impact through ownership, discipline, and vision.

OTHER RESOURCES

Atu and his business partners provide a variety of services that has a positive impact on communities. If you or someone in your community could benefit from their services don't hesitate to contact them.

Here's a list of their companies and contact info below:

CONTACT US TODAY!

—We want to help you on your journey to wealth.
If you have the money to invest in real estate, but lack the know how? We can help!

Contact us at:
www.legacyjourneygroup.com
(All you have to do is fill out the information request box, and we will contact you promptly.)

—We want to help you publish your next best-seller.
Are you an aspiring author, but need help bringing your book to publication? We can help!

Contact us at:
www.arpublishingco.com

COMING SOON!

—We want your office/commercial space to be pristine.
If you need a dependable, reliable commercial cleaning company to clean your office/commercial space? We can help!

Contact us at:
www.arbusinesscorp.com